Music & Movement

Rhona Whiteford & Jim Fitzsimmons

Bright Ideas
Early Years

Contents

Published by Scholastic Publications Ltd,
Villiers House, Clarendon Avenue,
Leamington Spa, Warwickshire CV32 5PR.

© 1991 Scholastic Publications Ltd

Reprinted 1992, 1993

Written by Rhona Whiteford and
Jim Fitzsimmons
Edited by Juliet Gladston
Sub-edited by Jackie Cunningham-Craig
Designed by Sue Limb
Illustrations by Jane Andrews
Photographs by: Martyn Chillmaid page
5
Chris Kelly pages 7 and 39
David Johnson page 23
Bob Bray pages 61 and 81
Cover by Martyn Chillmaid

Artwork by Norfolk House Graphics
Design
Printed in Great Britain by
The Alden Press Ltd, Oxford

British Library Cataloguing in Publication Data
Whiteford, Rhona
    Bright ideas for early years.
    Music and movement.
    1. Nursery schools. Teaching
    I. Title II. Fitzsimmons, Jim
    372.1102
ISBN 0-590-76402-0

All rights reserved. This book is sold subject to the condition
that it shall not, by way of trade or otherwise, be lent, hired
out or otherwise circulated without the publisher's prior
consent in any form of binding or cover other than that in
which it is published and without a similar condition, including
this condition, being imposed upon the subsequent purchaser.

No part of this publication may be reproduced, stored in a
retrieval system, or transmitted, in any form or by any means,
electronic, mechanical, photocopying, recording or otherwise,
without the prior permission of the publisher, except where
photocopying for educational purposes within a school or
other educational establishment is expressly permitted in the
text.

This book remains subject to copyright, although permission is
granted to copy pages 94–96 for distribution and use only in
the school or playgroup which has purchased this book.

Introduction

In the early stages of a child's development, music and the movement it inspires are often inseparable. At this stage the two 'disciplines' can and should be taught alongside each other. They often use the same concepts and vocabulary, and the activities common to each can be complementary. Indeed, there is tremendous potential in teaching the two in tandem.

A slight problem lies in the teaching adult's perception of the two disciplines. While many are prepared to 'have a go' when it comes to teaching movement and feel quite confident in encouraging body awareness, they often lack this vital confidence in teaching music and feel it is best left to those who have had a formal music training. We will show you that any good teacher of early years children, with an open mind and a great deal of enthusiasm, can make a significant contribution to the start of her children's musical education, and enjoy herself as well.

With the emphasis on exploration, expression, fun and enjoyment we have presented this book in the form of structured programmes and separate games to develop certain skills, so that you can dip into these to gain a little confidence in your own ability to teach. The best way to develop an approach to music and movement is to select an activity which you feel you can do and enjoy with your children, and then gradually to build up the range of activities that are suitable for their age and ability. When you feel confident, look at the more structured sections and plan your programme using these as guidance.

For the teacher of early years children many of the activities will be familiar from other contexts, so this book should be used as a support resource for those who have little or no experience in music and movement and wish to develop such a programme in their teaching.

The book is divided into sections on:
- developing listening skills;
- songs, stories and singing games;
- developing movement vocabulary;
- making sounds and music;
- making musical instruments;
- setting up a music corner and other useful resources.

The musical content has been kept very simple but structured on a sound curriculum basis.

Music is an integral part of life; most children are exposed to it from an early age and respond to it with varying degrees of vigour. Therefore, it is the teacher's task to try to give form to this experience and build upon it to develop children's awareness, appreciation, confidence and joy in movement and music.

Developing listening skills

Chapter one

The modern environment is filled with a kaleidoscopic array of sounds including a great variety of music. There is such a lot of music around us that often we stop listening to it and it merely becomes part of the general background noise. Also the visual impact of our world is so great that this too can distract us from listening. Therefore, it is important that we help our children learn to listen.

Listening and talking are basic skills in literacy, social development and music. The games and activities in this section are designed to interest the children in listening and to help develop their concentration. The children will be guided into simple sorting, matching, classifying, and movement activities and in working together.

The games can be played in any order, with small groups or the whole class, but they do require a quiet place so that there is maximum opportunity for concentration and listening.

Simon says

Age range
Three to four.

Objectives
To help children to listen for a start signal because music has specific starts and stops, and to connect symbols with actions.

What you need
Two plastic bottles, large coins, sand.

What to do
Put enough sand in one bottle to make an audible swishing sound when the bottle is tipped from side to side. Screw the lid on tightly. Do the same with the coins in the second bottle this time using enough coins to make a loud sound. Sit the children in front of you with a small barrier for you to operate behind so that they cannot see which bottle you are using.

This game has the same rules as 'Simon says', that is, the children must not do an action unless they hear a certain sound. If you rattle the coin bottle the children have to stand and if you shake the sand they must sit.

Follow-up
Vary the game by adding a third sound and action like clapping with arms in the air. The children can also take turns at being 'Simon'.

Big bangs

Age range
Three to four.

Objective
To encourage children to listen carefully for a cue.

What you need
Cardboard boxes, plastic buckets, pan lids, drums (real or home-made) table tops, the floor or anything which will give a loud noise when banged, assorted beaters such as wooden spoons, shoes, hands etc.

What to do
This is a game where the children are to be encouraged to make as big a noise as possible when they are given the cue. Let everyone have an 'instrument' and they can use their hands or beaters to make the noise. Make as much noise as

possible, but do be sensitive that more timid children may not like the noise level. Try letting them sit by you, or they may respond to the idea of having a go on their own or sharing an instrument.

Using the rhyme 'Five fat sausages', when you come to the place where you say, BANG! the children should try to make one big bang on their instruments and then keep them quiet until the next time. This may be the hardest bit! Encourage them to wait for the cue, slowing down your voice as you approach the, BANG, to create a sense of anticipation or try a whispered version with the children tapping their fingers on their palms for the BANG to give them a sense of contrast.

'Five fat sausages frying in a pan,
All of a sudden one went BANG!
Four fat sausages frying in a pan,
All of a sudden one went BANG!
Three fat sausages frying in a pan,
All of a sudden one went BANG!
Two fat sausages frying in a pan,
All of a sudden one went BANG!
One fat sausage frying all alone
That went BANG and then there were none!'

Shhh!

Age range
Three to six.

Objectives
To develop concentration and the ability to detect the tiniest sound. To help develop careful hand control.

What you need
A selection of noisy things such as bells, a packet of crisps, cymbals, maracas etc.

What to do
Working in a small group, sit round a table or on the carpet and pile the 'noisy things' in the middle so that they are all on top of each other.

The children can then take it in turns to try to extract a named item from the pile without any of the things making a noise. Vary the number and type of items included, depending on the ability of the children.

Encourage the children to be silent so that they can listen for the tiniest sound.

You can name the sounds, tinkle, rustle, swish, rattle, whoosh, clank etc. With older children invent sound words which resemble the sound like 'crik', for scrunched coloured transparent wrapping.

Loud and soft

Age range
Three to six.

Objectives
To recognise a range of volume in different instruments, and to practise making sounds in different volumes.

What you need
A variety of real and home-made instruments, for example, triangle, maracas, drum, recorder, guitar, chime bars. (NB You don't need to be able to play any of the instruments, as you will only be making sounds with them.)

What to do
Working with a small group or the whole class, start off by demonstrating the sound which can be made by several of the objects or instruments. The volume doesn't matter at this stage. Let the children have a go themselves.

Next, demonstrate the softest sound possible on the instruments. Try to produce sounds which are only just audible. Let the children try to do this and see who can produce the softest sound.

Now, trying each object or instrument in turn, let the children make as much noise as they can.

Follow-up
Have a competition to find which instrument or object can produce the softest sound and which the loudest.

Introduce vocabulary such as soft, gentle, faint, weak, loud, deafening, booming and piercing.

The Grand Old Duke and friends

Age range
Three to six.

Objective
To encourage the children to listen carefully to the words and silences in a rhyme.

What you need
A number of well-known rhymes.

What to do
Warm up by saying one or two rhymes together that everybody knows. Then start the game by singing 'The Grand Old Duke of York' but miss out the word 'up' each time it occurs. Leave a silence of the appropriate length to keep the rhythm and then carry on with the rhyme.

Other rhymes you can use are:
• 'Jack and Jill' leaving out 'Jack' or 'Jill'.
• 'Pussy cat, pussy cat where have you been?' leaving out 'cat'.
• 'Old Mother Hubbard' leaving out 'dog'.
Or the songs:
• 'If you're happy and you know it' leaving out 'happy'.
• 'John Brown's baby has a cold upon its chest' leaving out 'Brown', 'baby', 'cold', 'chest' etc.
• 'The wheels on the bus' leaving out 'bus', 'wheels' and 'day'.

Chinese whispers

Age range
Three to six.

Objectives
To help develop an aural memory and concentration.

What you need
A quiet place.

What to do
Sit in a circle and prepare the children for concentration by explaining that they have to listen very carefully as they are going to play a whispering game.

Think of a message and whisper it to the child next to you who must, in turn, whisper it to the one next to her and so on. Carry on until the message gets back to the child on your other side.

Make the message a simple instruction such as, 'Stand up and scratch your nose', 'Touch your toes', 'Stand on one leg' and so on. The final person to hear the message has to try to perform the instruction – if it is still in its original form!

Compare the original message and the final one, and play the game again, but start the message from a different place in the circle.

A listening walk

Age range
Three to six.

Objective
To develop children's awareness of the many sounds around them.

What you need
A tape-recorder if possible.

What to do
Prepare the children for a walk outside. Establish the idea before you go out that you are going for a listening walk so that the children must be as quiet as possible and listen carefully to everything. Tell them to try to remember the sounds they hear.

Go for a short walk round the school grounds, through the school itself, or around the neighbourhood. On your walk ask the children what sounds they can hear.

When you get back recap on what you have heard and together make a picture which shows all the sources of the sounds, such as a building site, lorry, bird, radio in a house, cars, running water, the wind blowing through trees and so on. Label the sound sources and invent words to represent the sounds, like 'zoosh', 'tick', and 'grrr'.

You can then go for another walk, and this time when you return try to classify the sounds into groups such as animal noises, human noises, traffic noises, land noises and air noises. It is helpful if you can take a tape-recorder with you to capture the sounds.

Everyday sounds

Age range
Three to five.

Objectives
To encourage the children to listen carefully to sounds, and to match them to their own experiences.

What you need
A portable tape-recorder, good quality recordings of about a dozen common everyday sounds from the home, for example, a vacuum cleaner, washing machine, telephone, a dog barking, a clock ticking, children laughing etc.

What to do
Sit the children in a quiet place and play the tape once or twice. Then ask the children to guess what the sounds are. Give heavy clues to help identification, as the sounds may be so familiar to the children in the home context that they cannot place them in isolation.

If possible ask the children to make short tapes of sounds from their homes — with parents' help, of course — which you can then listen to in another session.

Once the children have listened to the tape they can sit in silence for a few seconds and listen to the sounds which come from the rest of the school. Can they identify any?

Follow-up
Play 'sound lotto' using the tape and pictures of different objects. Each time the children recognise a sound they should cover the pictures of sound sources with numbered cards.

Match the sounds

Age range
Three to four.

Objective
To practise recognising sounds made by everyday objects.

What you need
Objects and pictures of the objects (for example, bunch of keys, paper, tin can, plastic carton, pencil, comb) mounted on a board, a box or screen.

What to do
Take one object at a time and make a sound with it. Then discuss these sounds with the children. Conceal the objects behind a screen or in a box and make the sounds again, one at a time.

The children have to listen carefully and try to recognise the sound, pointing to the correct picture.

Follow-up

Sit the children in a circle, get two of each of the objects and, keeping one for yourself, put the others in the centre of the circle. Let the children take turns using them in the following matching game:
● Choose one of your objects and make a sound with it. The child then has to match the sound by choosing the correct object from the centre of the circle and making the same sound.
● Try choosing two objects and make a sound with each. The child then has to match the sounds in the right order.

What do you think of this?

Age range
Three to six.

Objectives
To help the children to classify sounds, develop their aural and oral vocabulary, and their aesthetic awareness of sound.

What you need
Tape-recorder, tapes of everyday noises, music, sounds made by different musical instruments and different speaking voices.

What to do

Listen to each of the different recordings in turn, restricting it to a few minutes or a few sounds depending on the abilities of the children. Then discuss what you have heard, encouraging the children to try to classify the sounds in terms of loud, soft, quiet, low, deep, exciting, horrid, nice, nasty, gentle, fast, slow, frightening, lovely, soothing, sleepy, jumpy and so on.

The idea of this game is to ask the children to think about how they feel when they hear a sound and to express this as best they can. You should then offer further vocabulary to help them.

Shake a bit

Age range
Four to five.

Objective
To help develop children's listening skills by identifying a chosen sound from among a group of others.

What you need
Three jam-jars with screw lids; peas, rice and beads to put separately in each jar.

What to do
Sit in a circle with a small group of children and say a few nursery rhymes and poems as a warm-up. To play the game choose one of the jars and a part of the body which is good to shake, for example, the fingers, the feet, arms, or shoulders. Shake the jar and when the children hear the sound they must shake the chosen part of their body. Practise having silences and shakes. Once the children have had plenty of practice, say a poem or a nursery rhyme and at the end of a line shake the jar. The children are to shake each time they hear the sound. Vary the time you shake the jar.

Try several poems using different jars and picking different parts of the body to shake. Try to maintain interest and stop while everyone is still having fun.

Copy cats

Age range
Five to six.

Objective
To provide an opportunity for children to demonstrate physically their recognition of beat.

What you need
A selection of poems or nursery rhymes with a strong rhythmic beat.

What to do
Discuss with the children what sorts of noises can be made using different parts of the body. Then choose a simple nursery rhyme like 'Mary, Mary' or 'Simple Simon'. Say the rhyme and clap your hands in time to the rhythm. The children should listen for the first couple of recitations and watch you clapping in time. But when you shout 'Copy cats, copy that', the children should join in, clapping along in unison and in time to the beat. When the children have grasped the rhythm, you can make the sound with another part of the body — pat knees, snap fingers, tap feet etc.

By changing the nursery rhyme, different rhythms can be introduced and the children can be encouraged to clap along to the beat of their favourite songs.

As they gain in confidence and ability, individuals may be given the opportunity to be leader. You could also try clapping the rhythm of the children's names or foods like fish and chips. Can the children guess the names being clapped?

Follow-up

You can make up sequences for the children to copy, from a slow steady clap to more complex patterns and ones involving other parts of the body depending on the children's ability. For example, clap, snap, tap, clap, snap, tap. After a suitable period the listening skills may be enhanced by you sitting behind a screen and the children having to depend upon their experience of the sounds made, to enable them to repeat the sounds themselves.

In two groups, older children could try clapping and slapping different rhythms at the same time.

Pass it on

Age range

Five to six.

Objectives

To explore the sound-making possibilities of a range of percussion instruments, and to encourage the development of listening skills by identifying differences in the quality of sound.

What you need

A selection of untuned percussion instruments which have the potential to make a variety of sounds, for example, drum, cymbal, guiro.

What to do

Sit the children in a circle and give an instrument to one of the children in the group. Begin to clap a steady rhythm as the children pass the instrument from one to another round the circle. When you stop clapping the child holding the instrument has to make a sound with it.

Start clapping again as soon as the sound has been made and the children should pass the instrument round again. When the clapping stops this time, a different sound must be made from the instrument. You can help the children to make the sound at first and then ask questions like 'Was the sound the same as before?' or, 'How was that sound different?'

Encourage the children to think of unconventional ways of making sounds and other objects that can be used to create sounds, for example, a collection of small items such as brushes, strikers, ping-pong balls, beads or seeds may be placed in the centre of the circle within easy reach of the children. When all the possibilities have been exhausted, change the instrument.

Swing low/swing high

Age range
Five to six.

Objectives
To match sounds, and to distinguish between high and low notes.

What you need
A range of percussion instruments and two sets of chime bars, for example, two low 'A' and two high 'A' notes.

What to do
Let the children handle and explore the possibilities of sounds made by the percussion instruments. Choose five children giving four of the children a different instrument each while the fifth child has one instrument that matches one of the four held by the other children.

Sit the four children in a circle and blindfold the fifth one, putting him in the middle of the circle and turning him around.

Ask the four children to play their instruments at the same time and the fifth child to find the instrument that matches his own by turning towards the sound.

When the children have had plenty of practice in recognising sounds, take the chime bars and introduce the concept of high and low. You should have one set of high and low chime bars and a child has the other set. Strike the high note and then the low and see whether the child can copy this.

Strike two high notes again and ask the child to try to copy this.

This can be made more difficult by hiding one set of chimes while they are played so that the child really has to listen to the sequence. Finally, extend the

sequence of notes, for example, high, high, low, high, for the child to copy. This combination of notes can be varied to suit the individual's needs.

Finger shake

Age range
Four to five.

Objective
To encourage children to respond through selective listening to the sound or silence of an unseen instrument.

What you need
A screen to hide behind and a selection of instruments, for example, drums, bongos, tambourine, castanets.

What to do
Sit in front of the screen with the children. Choose an instrument, such as a drum, for yourself and a different instrument, such as castanets, for one of the children. The child then takes this instrument behind the screen. You start the game by playing a steady rhythm on the drum and the child behind the screen can choose when to start and stop playing the castanets.

As soon as the children hear the castanets they should hold up their hands and shake their fingers. The drum is to be played continuously while the child is behind the screen and when the castanets stop the rest of the children have to stop shaking their fingers.

The children will have to listen very carefully because the castanets can stop or start at any time. Listening to an instrument while another is being played continuously is very difficult for some children and it is even more difficult to notice when the instrument has stopped, so this game will need to be played quite often to develop the children's listening skills.

After a few minutes you can choose another child to go behind the screen with a different instrument.

Echoes

Age range
Four to six.

Objectives
To enable the children to recognise instrumental sounds, and to give each child the opportunity to play an instrument.

What you need
A collection of percussion instruments, one per child.

What to do
Make sure that the children have had a lot of experience using the instruments in an experimental way and that they know the names and recognise the sounds they make. Then make rhythmic patterns by beating out simple rhythms for example:
● 1 2, 1 2, 1 2
● 1 2 3, 1 2 3, 1 2 3 (emphasising the first beat)
● 1 2/3, 1 2/3, 1 2/3 (making the last two beats short)

The children then copy the beat on their instruments.

Over a short period of time a good vocabulary of rhythms and patterns can be built up.

Play it again

Age range
Five to six.

Objectives
To practise remembering rhythms, and to recognise instrumental sounds.

What you need
A blindfold and a collection of percussion instruments, one per child.

What to do
The children will need to practise playing the game 'Echoes' (above) before attempting this activity.

Sit or stand the children in a circle and give all except one of them an instrument. Blindfold the one without the instrument and stand him in the middle of the circle.

Choose one child to play a rhythm on her instrument. The blindfolded child must then try to guess the name of the instrument. If he is correct he takes off the

blindfold and takes the instrument from the child playing the sound. The children then shout, 'Play it again!' and he has to try to repeat the rhythm which has just been played. As he plays, get the other children to join in with their instruments.

Now the other child has to go to the centre of the circle and put on the blindfold. As soon as she is ready you, as the leader, raise an arm to stop the children playing. Then choose a different child to play his instrument and the blindfolded child has to guess which instrument it is and so the game continues.

It is important to remember to keep the rhythms very simple at first.

Traffic lights

Age range
Five to six.

Objective
To enable children to learn to distinguish between different musical sounds.

What you need
A selection of instruments and a screen to hide behind.

What to do
Choose three children to pick an instrument and go behind the screen. Ask them to play their instruments individually, and then two to play simultaneously. Ask one of the children to stop playing whenever she wants, and the rest of the group should try to indicate when they think this instrument has stopped by raising one hand.

When the group can do this reasonably well, introduce the third instrument. The children should play all

three together, each stopping at different times. The group again indicates when instruments have stopped being played with raised hands.

When you feel they have practised this enough, give each of the three instruments a colour using red, orange and green. The children then play their instruments simultaneously again, but this time when one of the children stops playing the rest of the children should identify the instrument not being played by calling out its colour.

Repeat this process a couple of times with a different instrument stopping each time, then change the children behind the screen and the game can start again.

Megaphones and echoes

Age range
Three to six.

Objective
To give the children experience of sound amplification and echoes.

What you need
A large sheet of stiff art paper, adhesive tape, felt-tipped pens, buckets, boxes, pans, card tubes, large empty containers.

What to do
Ask the children to make megaphones of different sizes from cones of stiff art paper and decorate them with felt-tipped pens before fixing the shape with adhesive tape. Let them test to see which size and shape of cone gives the best amplification of the voice and what is the furthest distance a child's voice can be heard with and without the megaphone. They can try normal speech, shouting and whispering. You may need to go into the playground for this as the amplification can be considerable. Older children will enjoy learning the new word, amplification, but for the youngest children merely refer to it as the sound being made bigger.

   The children can also try speaking into vessels of various sizes, for example, a bucket or a storage dustbin, to listen to the amplified sound. Most children recognise the sound and fun potential of an empty room or the school hall as soon as they enter it, so experiment with voice sounds here too.

   Echoes are produced in an empty space with hard surfaces when the sound is amplified and bounces off the surface back to the listener. Ask the children to try speaking into a plastic bucket, a metal

bucket, a cardboard box, or even a metal dustbin if possible, and see what happens to their voices. Ask the children to try out their voices in places they may visit with their parents such as a pedestrian tunnel, a cave, a station hall, a stairwell and a mountain valley.

Robots

Age range
Five to six.

Objectives
To practise listening carefully, and to follow instructions.

What you need
A large space to move in.

What to do
The children will need to have had experience of moving in a group and keeping as much as possible to within their own space.

Tell the children that they are all robots and you are the master controller. You are looking for the best one for a special mission, which can be in the form of whatever treat is currently popular in your class. They must obey all instructions immediately and if they fail they must go to the workshops, in other words they are 'out'. Then simply give them a variety of movements of different kinds, in single word commands, for example, stand, sit, run, stop, walk, skip, stop, turn, hop, walk etc. Put in plenty of 'stops' and keep the speed fairly slow to keep attention. You could also try speaking in an increasingly low voice to make the children concentrate on what you are saying. The game must be played in silence by the children.

Keep the game short and snappy and reduce numbers of players quickly so that those in the workshop are not left there too long.

'My music' quiz

Age range
Five to six.

Objective
To practise recognising different instruments.

What you need
A tape-recorder and a pre-recorded tape with 10 to 20 very short examples of different instruments which the children have heard before.

What to do
Organise the class into an audience and a panel of players, with you as the chairperson and score keeper and possibly a child as technician to work the tape-recorder. You can give the event a sense of occasion by having a signature tune and a 'glitzy' introduction.

Play a sound or tune for each player in turn. The children must try to guess what instrument or object is making the sound and you should give each child time to answer before going on to the next child.

You can award a point for a correct answer and let the audience guess any passes. It is a good idea to have the instruments you have recorded to hand so that you can demonstrate the sound if the children are completely stuck.

Developing movement to music

Chapter two

Music and movement go naturally together since they often share the same vocabulary and require a creative approach.

'Creative' does not simply mean 'free expression', even though the delight shown by young children in rhythmic movement can be seen at a very early stage. The task is to preserve this spontaneity and to provide opportunities for the children to develop an understanding and appreciation of what they are capable of in terms of movement, to enlarge their repertoire of expression and to try to encourage the linking of these movements to create simple sequences or movement passages performed alone, with a partner or in a group situation. Most young children will certainly be creative if left alone, but with help, there will be a tremendous improvement in the quality of their response.

Free expression should be allowed, but the children can be encouraged to select and sort movement by careful stimulation and guidance. Children always learn best by doing, and care should be taken to ensure that good effort is rewarded by praise, which will do much to stimulate, whereas criticism tends to depress young children.

It is a good idea to start in a fairly informal way by allowing the children to respond to music by moving. The more distinctive the sound and strength of rhythm, the more readily the children respond. The fact that their response is usually uncoordinated or lacking in quality is not important at this stage; the most important thing is that they feel the impulse to move, and it is your job to make that experience more meaningful.

Responding to music

Age range
Three to six.

Objective
To introduce the children to the connection between music, emotion and movement.

What you need
Recordings of different types of music: happy, jolly music, for example 'The snowman's dance' (Howard Blake) from *The Snowman* cartoon; slow, solemn music, for example, 'Song of the Volga Boatmen'; marching music, for example, *The Radetsky March* (Johann Strauss I) or *Marche Militaire* (Franz Schubert).

What to do
Ask the children to stand in a space in the hall and make sure they can stretch their arms in all directions without touching their neighbours. Now play the happy tune without giving the children any instructions. Observe how they react, noting which parts of their bodies they move. Some children may move their hands and arms, others their legs and feet and others a combination of these plus their heads. Still others may not respond at all. Playing only very short extracts, try the other musical pieces and observe reactions to these too.

Next, sit the children down and talk about emotions and feelings in a simple way, appropriate to their level of understanding. Give an example of how sound can affect the way we feel and react to a person speaking, or to what is being said. Make up a sentence, for example, 'Sit down quietly and cross your legs'. Say this in a gentle way with a quiet voice and then with an angry delivery in a loud voice. Ask which the children liked more and why, and which they did not like and why. Talk about how we show how we feel and ask the children to show that they are happy. Most will show it on their faces with a big smile. Ask them to show that they are sad, scared, surprised etc. Talk about how we show that we are happy with our bodies by jumping, waving arms, skipping, shaking heads. Play the happy music again and let the children do one or all of these things as the music plays.

Now talk about how we can show sadness or sorrow, possibly suggesting bowed heads, arms still, curled up body or rocking to and fro. Play the slow solemn music and let the children experiment with slow movements, heavy feet and slow walking.

Play the two pieces of music alternately and let the children move as they please. Praise and encourage the children who are moving in an appropriate way to each piece.

Introduce the marching music and see how the children respond to this. Do they need to move differently? Perhaps some of the children will have had experience of marching and will react in this way. Encourage them to march round the hall and the rest of the group will soon pick up their movements.

Over a period of weeks develop instinctive movement with lots of different types of music, simply for the experience of the different sound qualities and the variety of responses. The children will begin to develop a movement vocabulary.

Mix and match

Age range
Three to six.

Objective
To show that music can represent different things.

What you need
Two or three toys and instruments, for example, maracas and a toy snake; glockenspiel and a toy mouse.

What to do
Talk about how different things move and discuss with the children how they think various toys would move if they could and which instruments make a sound like the movement. Then hide the instruments from view and choose one and play it. The children are to listen and then shout the name of the toy it represents. Repeat this until they are familiar with each sound. Then you can ask the children to move in a way appropriate to the sound, for example, when you shake the maracas they are to move like the toy snake by sliding around the floor. A glissando on the glockenspiel as the striker is run up and down the bars should inspire the children to dart here and there just like the clockwork mouse.

You can play the instruments at random and mix the sounds one after the other and the children have to match their movements to the sound they hear.

They will need a lot of experience of this with as many different sounds and references to movements as possible. Encourage the children to take notice of the way in which things move and this will help them when they have to interpret the movements of particular objects or creatures with their own bodies.

What you need

Large drum, two metal dustbin lids, a small tin, a wooden beater or spoon, rick rack or rubbing board and maracas. Recorded music of light airy sounds, for example, 'Dance of the Sugar Plum Fairy' from *The Nutcracker Suite* (Tchaikovsky) and big, heavy sounds, for example, 'The Elephant' from *Carnival of the Animals* (Saint-Saëns).

What to do

Talk to the children about big things and little things, and try to decide which animals would take big steps and which would take little ones. Use words like big, little, enormous, gigantic, tiny, mini and huge.

Warm-up by asking the children to do huge jumps like a kangaroo and little jumps like a mouse. Encourage the children to spread out and use all the room available.

Next, using the large drum or the dustbin lids as cymbals, beat a slow steady rhythm and make as large a sound as you can while you march round with huge, spread out steps. Then do this again with the children.

Follow this by playing an instrument with a smaller sound, like the maracas, and this time move with tiny steps in different directions.

The children may confuse big sounds with slow movement and little sounds with quick movement, so try doing fast and slow movements for both types of sound. Also try some songs and nursery rhymes with movement in them, such as 'The Grand Old Duke of York' (march with big steps, then with little steps) or 'The wheels on the bus' (make tiny wheel movements with arms, then large ones) to contrast the sizes and translate them into movement.

Big and little

Age range
Three to four.

Objective
To develop a movement vocabulary, in this case thinking about size expressed by music and sound.

Action rhymes

Age range
Three to six.

Objective
To practise responding to a variety of sounds and music without prompting.

What you need
No special requirements.

What to do
Nursery rhymes and poems which incorporate actions are a good introduction to movement. The following are especially useful and good fun too:
- 'Incy Wincy Spider';
- 'Round and round the garden like a teddy bear';
- 'Five fat sausages';
- 'Row, row, row your boat';
- 'Pat-a-cake, pat-a-cake, baker's man';
- 'I'm a little tea pot short and stout'.

Poems, too, often lend themselves to mime. Try the following:
- I can tie my shoe lace,
I can brush my hair,
I can wash my hands and face;
And dry myself with care.
I can clean my teeth too,
And fasten up my frock,
I can say, 'How do you do?'
And pull up both my socks.

- Clap, clap hands, one two three
Put your hands upon your knee,
Lift them high to touch the sky,
Clap, clap hands and away they fly.

- Two little hands go clap, clap, clap,
Two little feet go tap, tap, tap,
Two little hands go thump, thump, thump,
Two little feet go jump, jump, jump,
One little body turns around,
One little child sits quietly down.

Stories with movement

Age range
Three to six.

Objectives
To involve the children in a movement story, and to develop concentration, listening skills and movement concepts.

What you need
A selection of musical instruments such as maracas, castanets, Swannee whistle, cymbals, tambourine, wood blocks etc. A recording of happy, joyous music and a selection of stories.

What to do
Devise simple narratives which involve playing instruments and doing actions to illustrate parts of the story.

Gather the children into a group or a circle around you and tell the story doing the sound effects and actions yourself. Then tell it again but this time ask the children to join in. Give them plenty of time to do a movement before stopping them and getting their attention to listen again. A good story to begin with is 'The Hare and the Tortoise'. In this story you can use maracas swished from side to side to illustrate the slow tortoise and castanets played quickly for the hare. The children can run around at the different speeds too. You can finish the story with some happy, joyful music with the children dancing anyway they please.

Follow-up
Try the story of 'Jack and the Beanstalk' using the following instruments:
• Swannee whistle for the growing beanstalk;
• Wooden blocks for climbing the beanstalk;
• Drum for the giant's footsteps;
• Tambourine for running away from the giant;
• Wooden blocks for chopping down the beanstalk;
• Maracas for the falling giant;
• Happy, joyful music at the end.

Body awareness
This can be developed through investigations of:
• movement and stillness;
• movement of specific body parts;
• whole body attitudes.

Stop and go

Age range
Three to six.

Objectives
To develop listening skills, to help children identify with the words 'stop' and 'go', and to help them understand when to start moving and when to stand still.

What you need
No special requirements.

What to do
Take the children into a large space where there is room to move. You should remember that stillness is to be looked upon as something positive and not just the absence of movement. It should be thought of as the position in which movement has just ended.

Ask the children to pretend to be statues and on the word 'stop', they must freeze and not move at all. When they hear the word 'go', they can move about on the spot, shaking hands arms and feet and they must listen for the word 'stop' and do so immediately they hear it.

This can be developed by asking the children to walk around the space, encouraging them to look for a space and avoid collisions. As they get used to moving around the space thoughtfully, they can run. The simple movement of running quickly and stopping abruptly will encourage self control in the children.

Follow-up
The theme of movement and stillness can be applied to other elements of locomotion which enable the children to travel along the floor, for example, stepping, running, rolling etc. The children can be introduced to moving their bodies in time to the sound of an instrument, so the starting and ending words may not be needed, the children taking their cues from the sound of the instrument.

Other elements of locomotion to be explored include hopping, skipping, leaping and jumping.

Variations in the basic possibilities of jumping are:
- from one foot to the same foot;
- from one foot to the other;
- from both feet, landing on one foot;
- jumping from one foot, landing on both feet.

These movements enable the body to travel upwards, to leave the floor and to fly up into or through the air. When jumping, the children will probably experience difficulty in landing so a little instruction in landing may be necessary (see 'Jump/freeze, on page 30).

Jump/freeze

Age range
Three to six.

Objective
To demonstrate a safe jumping and landing technique.

What you need
Tambourine.

What to do
Ask the children to jump up and down on the spot. Encourage them to bend their knees when they land so that they can absorb the shock. Repeat this a number of times until they can do it well.

Try all the different variations of jumping and give the children plenty of opportunity to jump and land. Give praise to those performing well and try to encourage those experiencing difficulty to follow the others' example.

When the children have mastered jumping and landing they will be ready for jump/freeze. For this activity shake the tambourine and this is the signal for the children to run around the space. When you strike the tambourine with a loud bang this is the signal for the children to jump high, land and then freeze their position.

Children can explore moving about the space using their feet and then explore the possibilities of moving in other ways, sliding, rolling, crawling. Encourage the opposites of moving and stillness with the children responding to commands or the sound of an instrument. The speed of movement can be varied using an instrument, for example, when the instrument is played fast, the children move quickly and vice versa.

Speed merchants

Age range
Three to six.

Objectives
To develop listening skills, and to encourage the children to move at different speeds in time to a beat.

What you need
Drum or tambourine.

What to do
Beat the drum slowly and ask the children to walk round the area available. After a while beat the drum more quickly and

ask the children to jog while looking out for spaces. Finally beat the drum as fast as you can and ask the children to run around, although they must be careful not to bump into others. You can then change the tempo at will and ask the children to respond immediately by moving at the correct speed.

To end the session, slow down the tempo until the children are moving more and more slowly until they stop. The children will need a lot of practice at stopping gradually, but it is worthwhile persevering as this will improve their listening skills and body awareness and control.

sides. They should move quickly on their toes, but slowly on their heels and sides.

Play the two instruments alternately with definite gaps between each one. Ask the children to listen to the sound and move accordingly at the right speed and take the appropriate steps, large or small. Encourage the children to move forwards, backwards, sideways, to lift their feet high or keep them close to the floor.

Play several short examples of recorded music with a slow, steady beat and with a quick, light beat so that the children can move in the way that they have learned but this time with the added excitement of a melody and different instruments.

Stepping stones

Age range
Three to six.

Objectives
To identify large and small steps, and use these movements with music.

What you need
Triangle, drum, recorded music with a slow, steady beat and a quick, light beat.

What to do
Bang a steady beat on the drum and ask the children to move about the space slowly, taking one big step with each beat of the drum. Give them lots of practice at this and reinforce the stopping and starting. Encourage them to keep still when the drum stops and move when the drum plays. Repeat this with the triangle but play it quickly and ask the children to take small quick steps in time to the sound. Encourage them to move on different parts of the foot; toes, heel,

Fiddle fingers

Age range
Three to six.

Objective
To explore movement with the fingers, hands, arms and shoulders.

What you need
An assortment of percussion instruments, examples of recorded music: fast, slow, light, heavy.

What to do
Ask the children to sit down in a circle or to spread out around the room and ask them to sit on their hands so that they cannot move them for the time being. Play several short examples of the music and the instruments you have, asking the children to listen, but also to think about their fingers, then hands, arms and shoulders.

Next, ask the children to show a range of movements with, in turn, their fingers, hands, wrists, elbows, arms and shoulders.

The children can practise without music and then try using music, fitting the quality of the music to the movement, for example, quick, light music can inspire quick shakes of the hands, quick wiggling of fingers or shoulders. Arms can be waved to slow music and so on. The idea is to get the children to concentrate on the part of the body they are using and relate this to the sound they are hearing in terms of quality.

When the children have had lots of experience of using and moving different parts of the body, opportunities may be given to allow them to explore moving in two very different ways concentrating on whole body action.

Rag doll

Age range
Three to six.

Objectives
To encourage observation and movement with whole body action.

What you need
Large, floppy rag doll, mechanical toy robot, Swannee whistle.

What to do
Using the rag doll as a visual aid, talk about how it can't stand up on its own. Show how the doll can be curled up in a

tight ball, and how it can be twisted and stretched into wide shapes and narrow shapes. Curl the doll into a tight ball and ask the children if they can curl up as tight as that; they will have fun trying. Open the doll up slowly so that it makes a wide stretched shape and ask the children to try to copy that too. Then hold the doll by the legs so that the upper body flops over, with the arms and head hanging loose. See if the children can experience the same feeling by letting their arms and body hang limply from the waist. Use the Swannee whistle to accompany their movements, they will enjoy the sliding sound as it almost mirrors the action.

Contrast this movement with that of the toy robot and see if the children can try to move in a stiff jerky way.

Follow-up
Look at other things to stimulate movement such as bubbles, balloons and the way elastic stretches. A piece of paper can be set to float down through the air, it can be crumpled up into a ball and then opened out slowly and smoothed flat.

Blowing up a balloon

Age range
Three to six.

Objective
To explore wide body shapes.

What you need
One large balloon.

What to do
Blow up a balloon so that the children can see the different stages – floppy balloon, slowly inflating balloon, slowly deflating balloon.

Ask the children to try to copy the balloon being inflated; first of all they are limp and lifeless as the air goes into different parts of their body. Then they start to stretch until they are blown up, after which they start to curl up as the air slowly escapes.

A variation of this is to let the children see what happens when the air escapes quickly from the balloon and this can lead on to moving through a space in different ways; rising and sinking, spinning, whirling round, using arms and legs to leap through the air and shaping movements with the body.

Awareness of time and weight

This can be developed through investigation of firm and fine touch, and quick and slow movements. An awareness of weight and time is important in movement so that children can observe the relationship between moving quickly or slowly and whether the time is long or short. Children enjoy the contrast of moving quickly and slowly. At first it is easier for the young child to move quickly because a slow movement needs more co-ordination and control. Much practice will be needed alternating slow and quick movements.

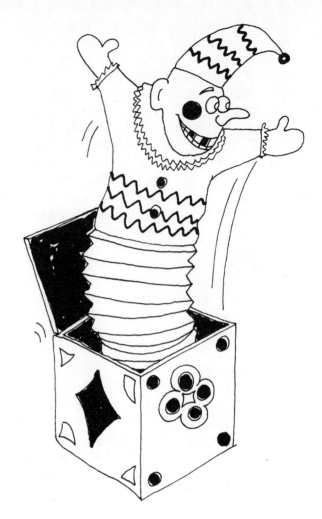

Jack-in-the-box

Age range
Three to six.

Objectives
To develop quick and slow movements, and to quicken reactions.

What you need
A Jack-in-the-box toy, a drum.

What to do
Together with the children watch the toy working. Then, in a space of their own, ask the children to crouch down on the floor, ready to spring, as they pretend to be the Jack-in-a-box, curled up tightly in his box with the lid shut. Bang on the drum; suddenly the lid is open and Jack leaps up stretching high in the air. Slowly he is pushed back down and the lid is closed again, but Jack is ready to spring as soon as the box is opened.

Follow-up
Ask the children to perform their range of movements quickly or slowly to develop their sense of speed and control, for example, run very fast, walk very slowly, raise your hands up to the ceiling quickly, slide your feet forwards and then sideways very slowly and so on.

Fairy footsteps and giant strides

Age range
Three to six.

Objectives
To develop concepts of heavy and light, and hard and soft.

What you need
An inflated balloon, a selection of instruments, for example, a triangle and drum.

What to do
The quality of weight in a movement depends on the amount of tension used in the muscles. Contrast such movements as punching, kicking and pressing with smooth and gentle movements, such as stroking, smoothing, floating and gliding. This can be done with or without musical accompaniment. The children will soon learn the difference between heavy and light.

An inflated balloon can again be used to show light and gentle movements as it is blown along the floor. Conversely ask the children to make heavy footsteps pressing down into the floor and alternate these with light, gentle steps which make no sound and hardly seem to touch the ground.

Awareness of space

This can be developed through investigations of:
- personal and general space;
- basic directions, spatial actions.

Children can explore space in many ways. The large area of space surrounding the body can be divided into six areas upper or lower, forwards or backwards, left or right. This is referred to as personal space. The different parts of the body can explore the different areas in front, behind, above and below and to the side.

Exploring space

Age range
Three to six.

Objective
To increase children's awareness of space.

What you need
No special requirements.

What to do
While standing still, the children can try to touch all the space in front of them as far as they can reach, then they can try to reach far out to the side, behind and so on. They can also explore these areas at different levels, for example, in front and low down or as high up as possible. All of their vocabulary of movements can be incorporated into this exercise, for example, 'stretch up high in front of you, reach down to the side'.

The floor, ceiling and walls can be used to help the children to direct their movements to a particular point, for example, 'Reach high above your head to the ceiling, stretch down low to touch the ground'. Or the directions may indicate a quality in the movement, for example, 'Stretch out your arm as straight as you can to touch the wall', or, 'Twist your arms and curl them down towards the floor'. Give the children plenty of practice at this and after a time they will be able to perform a series of movements directed to certain points based on straight, twisted or curved lines.

Three levels of movement make further divisions of space:
- High — up on the toes or jumping;
- Medium — this is the area between the shoulders and the hips most naturally used in turning;

● Deep – this is the area below the hips used by the legs, entered in crouching, sitting, kneeling, and lying.

Children who can move through these three levels as they travel around a space, rising and sinking and exploring the space around them in a straight, angular, curved or twisted path, will have developed a considerable movement vocabulary.

The nature of the path taken in space will develop in the children a sense of relationship with the rest of the group since there will be an awareness of where they are in the group.

Finding space

Age range
Three to six.

Objective
To develop an awareness of proximity to other children and adequate space for movement.

What you need
A large space.

What to do
The children start this activity standing in their own space. You can then encourage them to move around the space, look for new spaces and to move continually into them. When you stop them, each child should ideally be in a space of their own again.

As the children are moving around, encourage them to change direction and take different pathways, curved, straight and twisting. They can carry on going straight until they meet an obstacle, either a wall or another child, then they should change direction by turning around and carrying on in a straight line again. As

before, the idea is for the children to be alone in a space when you say, 'stop'.

A variation of this is for the children to work with a partner. They can decide who is to be, 'number one,' and, 'number two'. Number two is to follow number one, who walks around the space, and has to keep so close that when you say stop she can reach out and touch number one. Bumping is not allowed.

Partner work

This can be developed through investigation of:
- alternate movement;
- simultaneous movement.

Mirror, mirror

Age range
Three to six.

Objectives
To encourage observation, body awareness, and a relationship with a partner or a group.

What you need
A large space.

What to do
Ask the children to choose a partner, find a space to work in and then stand facing each other. The children can then decide who is to be 'one' and who is 'two'. They are to stand in their places for this activity. Ask the 'ones' to start moving and the 'twos' to watch closely and try to mirror everything the 'ones' do.

The children may move hands, wrists, arms, shoulders and heads. They may bend at the waist, twist and turn, stretch and curl but they must keep their feet as still as they can. With twisting and turning it is advisable that they stand with their feet slightly apart in order to keep their balance. They must face their partner so that each move they make can be easily seen and if they move steadily without sudden movements the partner has time to mirror the action easily. Let partners swap roles after a while.

It is important to remember that the development from random movements does not only come from vigorous exhausting activity, but also from small delicate movements which are just as valuable providing the children are concentrating. Just how the children move from one position to another is as important as getting there and the different ways need to be suggested over and over again.

Making sound and music

Chapter three

Before embarking on the more structured approach of learning how to accompany songs and how to create music on their own, it would greatly benefit the children if they had some experience of developing listening skills, some feel of music through movement and some experience of singing.

The early part of this chapter suggests ways of widening the children's general experience of sound through other areas of the curriculum; their play, art and craft, language and science. At the end of the chapter there is a selection of games, which can be dipped into at will, that foster the social skills needed in music, such as co-operation.

The important thing to remember is to look at the needs of the children in your care and decide from which point it is best for you to start.

39

the children or at least display a picture of it.

• Using any topic as a starting point get the children to make or paint pictures and then try to produce sounds to fit the pictures. For instance the children could make collages of monsters and then invent voices for them using the instruments. You could do this as a group activity so that everyone could help each other. Display a selection of pictures and put the instruments within easy reach of the children.

• Take a simple story line such as '. . . going out to play . . . it starts to rain . . . puddles appear . . . jumping in the puddles . . . clothes all dripping wet . . . running home . . . meeting Mum!'

With the children in a circle, and a selection of instruments in the middle, decide which instruments can illustrate each part of the story, where they fit in to the story and how long each should be played; for example, you may want three or four 'splashes' with cymbals. As the children get more experienced sounds can appear simultaneously, one can fade and so on.

To translate this into a pictorial yet linear form is the next step so that the children can see music represented in 'notation' and play it again using the 'score'. It is also a valuable exercise in imagery and sequencing. All you do is provide a long piece of paper and some felt-tipped pens or crayons and starting at the beginning of the events draw some symbols to represent each sound putting them in a linear sequence. There will be much useful discussion needed to decide what symbols are best to represent each sound. Should it be diagonal slashes or zigzags to represent the rick rack rain sound?

Write underneath what each symbol represents, to add to the sight vocabulary and also to jog the memory.

Many other topics lend themselves to

this treatment:
• a machine working,
• a storm at sea,
• getting up in the morning,
• making a cake,
• a train journey,
• a bird flying,
• a bee flying,
• a sudden fog,
• a magic spell,
• a ride on a roundabout,
• the park.

Sound experiments

Age range
Three to six.

Objective
To examine the production of sound.

What you need
An assortment of instruments (wind, string, tuned and untuned percussion) a tuning fork, a bowl of water, elastic bands, comb and paper, rice paper bits, ruler.

What to do
There are basically three types of instruments: percussion which can be tuned or untuned and are shaken or banged; wind which are blown; and stringed which are strummed or plucked.

Sound is produced from these instruments in a variety of ways but in each case it is caused by vibrations and you can show this to the children with a few simple experiments.

Using your collection of instruments let the children experiment with playing them and see if they can discover how the sound is produced and sort them into three sets; banged, plucked and shaken.

Encourage the children to feel the instrument as it is played. They will easily feel the vibrations as a piano is played (take the back off so that they can see that the strings are banged) or see the strings of a guitar moving.

Some other experiments which the children could do to feel vibrations are as follows:
- If they use a paper and comb kazoo or paper-straw pipes (see page 76), they will feel the vibrations on their lips or in the pipes as they blow.
- Tap a tuning fork on a hard surface. The children can listen to the sound and actually see the vibrations it produces by placing the tip on the surface of a bowl of water and watching the water ripple.
- Put rice or small pieces of paper on to a wide topped drum and then tap the drum with a beater. The children can watch the rice or paper jump with the vibrations.
- Pluck the strings of an elastic band guitar (see page 78) and watch them vibrate.
- Hold a ruler firmly on the edge of the table and pull it down then let go. Try different lengths of ruler over the edge to see whether you get a different sound and a different quality of vibration.
- Tap a length of central heating pipe with a metal beater at one end and let the children put their ears to the pipe a distance away. Can the sound be felt or heard?

Pitch refers to how high or low a musical note is, and in terms of the physics of music, the faster the vibration, the higher the note and the slower the vibration the lower the note. This can be demonstrated by the following means:
- If you shorten the vibrating string of a

guitar, you make the vibrations faster and so a higher note is produced. Use one finger to hold the string on the fretboard, and another to pluck the string. Move the clamping finger down the string and let the children listen to the note going higher and higher.

• Play with a xylophone or a glockenspiel, and look at the size of the bars compared to the sound.

• Show the children how the holes on a recorder, when all covered up, produce a long tube and the note is low. Show that by uncovering holes the tube is shortened and the note is higher. Make different lengths of straw pipes to show this in a more concrete way for younger children.

When the children have had some experience of playing tuned instruments introduce them to different *qualities of sound* in the same note played on different instruments. An 'A' on a glockenspiel will sound different in character to an 'A' played on a xylophone or on a piano. The pitch of the note may vary, it may be a high or a lower note but the notes will have a different character which will be more suited to one tune or another. For example, a song about skeletons dancing will be best accompanied by a xylophone as this sound will help paint the picture of bones rattling better than the tinkling sound of a glockenspiel.

Joining in with songs and poems

Age range
Three to six.

Objective
To introduce the children to making music by feeling the rhythm with their bodies.

What you need
A repertoire of songs and poems.

What to do
This activity requires the use of the commonest instrument of all – the body! The children can actually feel the rhythm of the song or poem if they join in with clapping hands, thumping fists, tapping feet, clicking fingers, slapping knees or even making vocal sounds. They will actually become part of the music. You will get the hang of the words, music and the actions. Do three or four well-known songs or rhymes each session and only introduce a new song every other session, depending on the receptivity of the children. Any poems or songs you choose need to have plenty of action, preferably of a repetitive nature, so that there are lots of clap, clap, claps, or tap, tap, taps.

For example, songs and verses where the sound is spoken as part of the rhyme:
● I can knock with my two hands;
Knock, knock, knock!
I can rock with my two hands;
Rock, rock, rock!
I can tap with my two hands;
Tap, tap, tap!
I can clap with my two hands;
Clap, clap, clap!

You and the children can always think of more lines to this rhyme, for example, stamp, thump, nod etc.

Try also the following:
● 'Peter hammers with one hammer';
● 'Let your hands go loudly clap, clap, clap';
● 'Ten fat sausages sitting in the pan';
● 'The wheels on the bus go round and round' (the children can make circular movements with their hands for the wheels and clap to 'All day long').

These are all available in *This Little Puffin . . .* compiled by Elizabeth Matterson (Puffin Books).

Using instruments with finger rhymes and action songs

Age range
Three to six.

Objectives
To introduce the use of instruments, and to give the children the opportunity to contribute to a sound picture.

What you need
A selection of instruments which the children have played with before.

What to do
The children should be quite familiar with nursery rhymes and many of the common action songs so it will be a short step for you to introduce musical sound to emphasise different characters or actions or stages in the story line. For example:
● Five currant buns in a baker's shop,
(Bang on drum)
Round and fat with sugar on the top.
(Maracas on 'sugar')
Along came a boy with a penny one day,
(Triangle on the last three words)
Bought a currant bun and took it away.
(Bang on drum)

● Slowly, slowly, very slowly
(Gentle maracas on this line)
Creeps the garden snail.
Slowly, slowly, very slowly
(Gentle maracas on this line)
Up the wooden rail.
Quickly, quickly, very quickly
(Run on glockenspiel on this line)
Runs the little mouse.
Quickly, quickly, very quickly
(Run on glockenspiel on this line)
Round about the house.

- Five little froggies sitting on a well;
(Clappers on 'froggies')
One looked up and down he fell;
(Bang drum on 'fell')
Froggies jumped high;
(Bells on 'high')
Froggies jumped low;
(Tambourine on 'low')
Four little froggies dancing to and fro.
(Continue the song until there are no
froggies left.)

All these verses and more can be
found in the invaluable *This little Puffin* . . .

Stories with sound effects

Age range
Three to six.

Objective
To add another dramatic dimension to a
story, and to give the children practice in
handling instruments for a purpose.

What you need
A selection of instruments, 'real' and
home-made.

What to do
Choose some favourite stories which the
children have heard before and add
sound effects where the story line
suggests. At first you can indicate where
a sound may be useful and then
encourage the children to pick an
instrument to illustrate the action. After
they have had a little practice the
children will begin to form their own
ideas about where a sound is needed.
Not all stories lend themselves to sound
effects but the following are good ones
to use with young children.
- 'The little Gingerbread man' – use
maracas to accompany the Gingerbread
man's repeated cry of, 'run, run as fast as
you can, you can't catch me I'm the
Gingerbread man!' Coconut halves can
be used as the footsteps of the old man
and the old woman, a small drum for the
cow and bells for the dog's feet and so
on.
- 'Goldilocks and the three bears' – use
the piano to accompany the different
voices of the bears, simply playing two or
three notes in a row for each bear; low
for father bear, middle octaves for
mother and high for baby bear. Play a
single note in time to the words, like
'Who's been eating my porridge?'.

- 'The little red hen' — use maracas for the little hen pecking at the corn and for whenever the little hen 'carries on working'. You could pick a different instrument for each of the other animals to underline their constant cries of 'Oh, no, not I'.
- 'The owl and the pussy cat' — use gently swished maracas for the sound of the sea, the highest three strings of a guitar plucked for the owl's song to pussy, a deep drum banged for the tree, bells for the money, a triangle tinged gently for the 'stars above'. Some sounds can be played once on the word which needs illustration and others such as the sea noises can be continuous under the narrative.

Follow-up
Write out a story in large print and wherever you have used a sound effect include this in the text by showing a symbol. The children can then read the story for themselves and add the sound effect at the right place. They would also enjoy simply reading the story and trying to make a sound effect orally. They can be quite inventive when asked to make a sound like falling bricks with their mouths!

Clap the rhythm

Age range
Three to six.

Objective
To give the children experience of a range of rhythm patterns.

What you need
No special requirements.

What to do
Regular, short sessions of rhythmic clapping can greatly develop the children's sense of rhythm. With the youngest children, just clap a short pattern of three or four beats, emphasising the first beat, and repeat it four or five times. Then ask the children to join in. When they have the idea, switch to another pattern. Then you can build in some other ways of marking the rhythm, by patting knees, tapping feet, and so on. Children will also enjoy clapping out the rhythms of their names, and of favourite food words, such as fish and chips or baked beans.

With older children, try clapping along to the rhythm of a simple song, perhaps using alternate hand claps and slaps of the knees. When they have mastered this, divide them into two groups and start one group off clapping in one rhythm, for example:
1 2 3 4/4   1 2 3 4/4   1 2 3 4/4
Then start the other group off clicking fingers or slapping knees to a different rhythm, so that the two rhythms rum simultaneously:
1 2/2 3 4   1 2/2 3 4   1 2/2 3 4
In activities of this kind it is always best to decide on a starting and stopping signal before you begin! The children will need plenty of practice with starting and stopping, so make it fun.

'Orchestra' training

Age range
Four to six.

Objectives
To introduce the children to following a leader, and to playing instruments together in a large group.

What you need
A selection of percussion instruments, 'real' and home-made.

What to do
Use percussion instruments at first, as shaking and banging these instruments is easier for the younger child than blowing or plucking and strumming. Do make sure that there is an instrument for everyone and if practical in your situation, try to limit the number of children to about 20. You will also find it advantageous to limit the number of loud items like big drums as they can easily drown the whole proceedings. Easy instruments for initial sessions include things like scrapers, shakers, and small drums. You are initially going to accustom the children to follow signals which tell them to play and to stop and also indicate different ways of playing, like loud, soft, quick, slow. You need to think of signals for each of these things.

You also need to insist on a certain regime during these sessions, as music does require an element of control. Always use the same hand signals so that the children can rely on them and start the sessions with the instruments silent, until everyone is ready, but don't keep them hanging on for too long as the strain may well be intolerable.

The first thing to do is to let the children have experience of a conductor. Show them the signals and try them all out, emphasising the 'stop' signal. You can then devise a series of experiences, such as 'Everyone play loudly, then stop' followed by 'Everyone play quietly, then stop', or vice versa.

Repeat each item several times so that the children gain confidence but try to keep the session fairly short to maintain children's interest. Organise different groups of instruments to be played on their own for a short recital. You can make it into a learning game by seeing which group can play the quietest or the loudest.

Introduce the idea of playing along to songs. Choose well-known nursery rhymes, as they have easy tunes without much variation, and simply decide beforehand how you will all play — loudly or softly. Let the children 'play' along, with complete freedom to your singing and they can join in if they can. Don't forget the signal for playing and stopping. You can also play songs quickly or slowly. Try singing them with the children without instruments so that they get the hang of the different speeds.

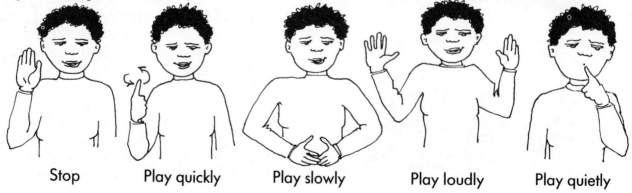

Stop   Play quickly   Play slowly   Play loudly   Play quietly

After some practice you can introduce new and more difficult elements, for example, getting louder and getting softer. Devise your own signals and practice them in a separate session.

Follow-up
The children will enjoy these combinations once they have had some practice in the basic skills: play loudly and quickly; play loudly and slowly; play quietly and quickly; play quietly and slowly; play loudly then get quieter; and play fast then get slower.

If you keep the sessions short and well controlled with the children used to keeping their instruments quiet when not in use, then you will quickly establish a good basis for further learning.

Accompanying songs with untuned percussion instruments

Age range
Four to six.

Objective
To introduce the children to accompaniment of songs in a more structured way, using untuned percussion instruments.

What you need
A selection of untuned percussion instruments, for example drums, clappers, maracas and bells.

What to do
Start off with short and simple songs which are quite repetitive. It is worthwhile looking out a small repertoire of songs before you start. However, don't let the songs become a dirge; approach them with energy, at a fair pace, and keep the sessions short and snappy and if possible very regular. Young children respond to quick enthusiasm and energy.

Indeed, the children's own enthusiasm may well drown a song, so at first only use one or two instruments which can be passed round, and the rest of the class can pretend to play an instrument of their choice.

Show the children how to hold and play the various instruments.

Songs with a sound in the words
Start off with songs which have a sound in the words. Use untuned percussion instruments, as they are the easiest to use when first learning to accompany songs, but most importantly the sound of these

instruments does not interfere with the tune of a song and can therefore produce a pleasing combination.

'We can play on the big bass drum
And this is the music to it;
Boom, boom, boom goes the big bass drum
And that is the way we do it'.

This song is ideal as the children can join in on the 'boom, boom, boom'. Other verses can be invented to suit the instruments you have. At this stage try to get the children to keep to the three beats of the 'boom, boom, boom' so that they keep in time to the music. Adapt other songs to suit your needs.

Songs with actions

The children can then move on to accompanying songs such as the following examples:

- 'If you're happy and you know it clap your hands'. Here the children can use the instruments to accompany the two beats of 'clap, clap'. Pick instruments to illustrate the action, for instance use a drum for 'Nod your head' or the bells for 'Shake your legs'.
- 'Heads and shoulders, knees and toes'. In this song they can use one shake of the maracas for each word in 'knees and toes'. Older children who have had a fair bit of practice can try using one instrument to accompany each of the different body parts.
- 'Incy Wincy Spider'. Here they can use clappers or coconuts to beat out the rhythm of the spider climbing, maracas for the rain, a cymbal on the word 'washed', a continuous run on the glockenspiel for the sunshine and more maracas to represent the spider climbing again.

Other suitable songs include:
- 'The farmer's in his den';
- 'Here we go round the mulberry bush';
- 'The hokey cokey';

- 'I'm a little teapot';
- 'One finger, one thumb, one hand';
- 'One two, buckle my shoe';
- 'Frère Jacques'.

Songs with a chorus

Once the children have experience of using instruments which have a particular character to suit the mood of a song, you can progress to more difficult songs which are longer and have a chorus although you should first discuss which instrument will most enhance the mood of the song. Possible songs include 'The Grand Old Duke of York', 'Bobby Shaftoe', 'Mr Noah', 'Daisy, Daisy' and 'Jingle Bells'.

Most choruses have very definite, easy rhythms which can be easily accompanied. You can simply get most of the children to clap along to the rhythm of the chorus and give instruments to two or three. It is best to add a few

instruments at a time until you gain confidence as the conductor. If you haven't got the music to see how many beats there are in a bar, listen carefully and try to work it out, so that you can clap to every beat or every other beat etc.

You can use one instrument to beat out the main rhythms of the song throughout the verses and chorus and add other instruments in the chorus. Children who haven't got an instrument can help the music with claps, slaps, finger clicks and palm taps etc. Sometimes vocal accompaniment suits the song, such as a backing of swish, swish, swish to a song about the sea as a rhythmic backing, although the rhythm must be that of the song.

Accompanying songs with tuned percussion instruments

Age range
Five to six.

Objective
To introduce the children to accompaniment of songs in a structured way using tuned percussion instruments.

What you need
A selection of tuned percussion instruments, for example, glockenspiels, chime bars and xylophones.

What to do
When the children start to accompany songs using instruments which are pitched, that is, which can produce notes, care has to be taken that the notes fit in with the song. The easiest way of doing this is to start off with short rhythmic patterns which use the notes in the song. These are called ostinati. An ostinato is a little repeating pattern of two, three or four notes which are chosen from the tune and which continue throughout the song. This can sound delightful and even a two note pattern can be easily learned and will give a marvellous sense of achievement. Once the children can keep up a rhythm with untuned percussion instruments, it is time to introduce ostinati with tuned percussion instruments like metalaphones, glockenspiels, xylophones or chime bars. The ostinato accompaniment is started at the same time as the song and the rhythm is kept up throughout.

Try 'Lavender's blue' using the notes 'DGA' played throughout or 'Dance to your daddy' using 'DGA' or 'Oranges and lemons' using 'FCC' for each bar in the first and second lines, 'CGG' for each bar in the third line and 'FCC' again for the last line. See photocopiable pages 94–96 for some simple ostinato fitted into tunes for you. When in doubt follow the guitar chords often marked above the stave. In the case of chords with modifications like 'G$_7$' or 'Am' try 'G' or 'A' and decide whether this sounds right — be adventurous!

Simple tunes to play on tuned percussion instruments

Age range
Five to six.

Objective
To enable children to play short phrases from tunes.

What you need
A selection of tuned percussion instruments, for example, chime bars, glockenspiels etc.

What to do
As a simple introduction to playing tuned instruments of any kind the children will enjoy playing little phrases from well-known songs and nursery rhymes. Start with short phrases and build up, as when learning to read words.

Some songs will require the use of sharps (#) and flats (b), and these notes need to be pointed out to the children. Let them hear the difference and identify them visually on the instrument. You will usually find two sets of notes (octaves) on a glockenspiel, for instance; one of the lower-sounding version and one high. So you will have a high 'C' note (written here with a (') next to the note) and a low 'C' (written as C).

Try out some of the following:

- This old man
  G E G
- London's burning
  C   C   F   F
- Pat-a-cake
  C D G

(from 'Pat-a-cake, pat-a-cake baker's man')

- Incy Wincy spider
  G G G A B B
- One man went to mow, went to mow
  B B B   B B   B   C C

a meadow
B B A

- Three blind mice (twice),
  C   G   C

see how they run
G F F   E

- One, two, three, four, five
  B   B   A   G   G
- Oh, do the hokey cokey
  A   G F D C   D F
- The wheels on the bus go round and
  C F   F F F A C   A

round
F

- Here we go round the mulberry bush
  F   F   F   F   A C A   F

52

- If you're happy and you know it
  D D G G G G G G

clap your hands
F G A

- The farmer's in his den, the
  C F F   F F F G

farmer's in his den
A A A A A

- Heads and shoulders, knees and
  G   A G F# G

toes, knees and toes
E G G

- I'm a little teapot, short and
  C D E F G C' A   C'

stout
G

Some children will be able to pick out the rest of the tunes themselves, and you could get them to write them down for the other children.

Follow-up

The children will enjoy creating their own tunes using the tuned percussion instruments. Chime bars, glockenspiels and xylophones, with removable notes, are the most practical instruments to use as you can limit the number of notes available.

You can make a scale on the note of C which is within the singing range of young voices. This is called a *pentatonic* scale which in this case are the notes: C D E G A C'.

Start off by making up rhythmic tunes of two notes using the following starting points:

- Use the children's names; for example, Susan Laura Stephanie
      G A   A C   C G C'

The children should say the word and play the notes and then sing the word.

- Play echoing games where you play a phrase, for example, Hello
                       E D

and the children have to echo it on their own instrument. They can then make up phrases themselves, making them longer each time.

- Play question and answer and ask the children to sing out their question as they play it, for example, Who are you?
                 C A G

The other children can answer in the same way.

- Play slowly, quickly, quietly and loudly. Try different beaters on the different instruments to listen to the changing sound quality.

Games

None of the games and activities in this section require any specialist musical knowledge, merely the skills of a good teacher. These games are designed to develop skills of listening, concentration, interaction and to some extent expression. Most games are intended for work with groups and since most also involve a fair bit of noise, care must be taken not to disturb others.

The games are not in any way formal music lessons but played with enthusiasm they will certainly encourage in the children a love of musical sound and an opportunity for free expression, creativity and the development of social skills.

Through the medium of play the children find out about the range of possibilities for making sound without any of the pressures of being right or wrong, the emphasis being on having fun and becoming totally involved and engrossed.

The games are not an end in themselves but rather a means to an end. They are intended as a means of gaining confidence with basic music elements and materials. The children will have experience of playing different instruments and of discovering the different sounds they can produce. They will also gain experience of elementary concepts such as tempo (fast/slow), pitch (high/low) and volume (loud/soft).

Musical pairs

Age range
Five to six.

Objectives
To practise matching sounds and the social skill of taking turns.

What you need
A selection of instruments, two of each kind.

What to do
Split the children into two groups and sit them back to back and give them an identical selection of instruments. Then ask one child from the first group to choose an instrument and make a sound with it. The second group, in consultation with each other, have to decide which instrument was used and make a sound on the same instrument in their set. If they are correct then they win a point.

Now someone from the second group has to choose an instrument while the first group listens carefully. They then respond in the same way and if they guess correctly they win a point and so the points build up with each group taking turns. (Some children will find it difficult not to peep, so you can award penalty points to prevent this.) For older or more competent children the game can be made more difficult by asking that the rhythm used by one group is copied by the second.

All join in

Age range
Five to six.

Objectives
To encourage careful listening and free expression.

What you need
A selection of instruments, enough for each child and yourself.

What to do
The children sit in a group in front of you with their chosen instruments and you choose two instruments which are very different, such as a triangle and drum.

Put a low barrier in front of you so that the children cannot see which instrument you are playing, and decide together which of your instruments represent 'all join in' and which means 'keep quiet'. Now you can play your instruments alternately for short periods, and when the 'all join in' instrument is played the children should join in with theirs, playing as they like until you change to the other. They must watch you and listen carefully to take their cue.

As they get used to the game the children can play on their own with one of the children acting as leader while you watch.

Rhythm relay

Age range
Five to six.

Objectives
To develop concentration, auditory memory and control.

What you need
One fairly small and quiet instrument for each child.

What to do
Divide the children into groups of equal size and arrange each group into a line as for a relay race, with the children standing one behind the other holding their instruments. Make sure there is a good space between each group and between each child.

The first child in each line should then come to you to hear you beat out a short, simple, secret rhythm on an instrument. The rest of the children should not be able to see or hear it. The children then return to their places and at a signal from you run to the next child in the line and play the rhythm. They must do it secretly and quietly so that the other groups do not see or hear it.

Each child then passes the rhythm to the next child in the line until the last child in the group has got the rhythm. The last children then race to the front of their lines and the first group to do this raise their hands and have the first chance to play the rhythm to the rest of the class. This group will have to decide who is going to represent them and play the rhythm. If it is played correctly they are the winners. If it is not correct then the other groups can try until the winners are found.

Keep this activity very controlled but fast moving and fun.

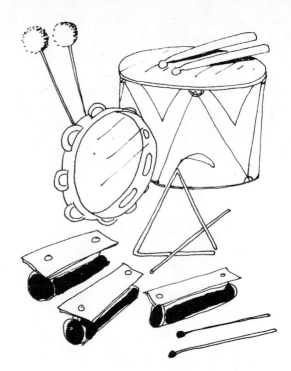

Add a rhythm

Age range
Five to six.

Objective
To develop auditory memory.

What you need
A selection of instruments.

What to do
Work with a small group and sit the children in a circle and let each one select an instrument. Ask each of them to make up their own short rhythm and practise it to fix it in their minds. Everyone will have to keep to a reasonable noise level!

When the children are ready, ask one of them to start by playing their rhythm just once and the next child then has to copy this rhythm and add another one.

The next child has to try to play both these rhythms and add another. The object is to see how many rhythms can be remembered by one child. This is difficult but the children will improve with practice. However, you will need to make sure that you give everyone the chance of starting off so that the same children are not always faced with the longest collection of rhythms.

Sounds in a story

Age range
Three to six.

Objectives
To develop imagination and confidence.

What you need
A selection of percussion instruments.

What to do
Sit the children in a circle with the instruments in the centre and easily accessible to all. Choose the instruments to suit the story, offering several alternatives.

The children will listen to you telling the story, and at appropriate points can take it in turns to pick up an instrument to provide a suitable sound effect. The story can be as simple as you like; for example:

'One day I was walking down the road, and I heard the bell ringing on the town hall (*triangle*). Coming down the road was a horse (*coconuts*). It was pulling a cart covered with bells (*handbells*) . . .' and so on.

Pass the hat

Age range
Three to six.

Objective
To develop self-confidence.

What you need
A hat and a range of instruments.

What to do
Sit the children in a circle with their hands on their knees. Then choose a song with

which everyone is familiar, and get the children to join in singing with you while the hat is passed round the circle. The child who has the hat on the last word of the song has to leave the circle, take a musical instrument and accompany the next song in any way she likes. A new song can be chosen each time so that the children have plenty of variety and older ones will not be able to predict who is likely to have the hat at the end.

You can either let the children return to the circle after they have had a go with an instrument (try to make sure the hat doesn't land on the same child twice) or you can let the number of children with instruments accumulate until there is one child left passing the hat; then that child is declared the winner.

Blind man's buff

Age range
Five to six.

Objectives
To help develop confidence, group co-operation, handling of instruments and the concept of volume and aural concentration.

What you need
A blindfold and a collection of different instruments.

What to do
You will need to find a large space to work in. Choose two children, one to be blindfolded and one to be a static goal. The rest of the children should each have an instrument which they use to guide the blindfolded child to the goal. The children can play the instruments in any fashion, the only guide being that they must watch the blindfolded child and play their

instruments very slowly if she is moving away from the goal and quickly if she is near.

The children will need to practise the speeding up and slowing down before the child puts the blindfold on and you will need to make sure the area is clear so that there is little likelihood of bumps.

As soon as the goal is found two more children can take over and the first two join in with playing the instruments.

You can ask the children to play their instruments loudly and softly to vary the game and maintain interest.

Which way now?

Age range
Five to six.

Objectives
To help develop self confidence, concentration and co-operation.

What you need
A blindfold and a selection of instruments, one for each child.

What to do

You will need a large area like the hall. For this game one child is chosen to be blindfolded and the other children stand in their own space not too close to anyone else, holding their instruments in their hands.

The object of the game is for the blindfolded child to make his way across the room, through the other children without bumping or touching them. You can provide a goal by standing at the other end of the room.

As the blindfolded child approaches, the children use their instruments to make a small warning sound. The only rule is that the blindfolded child should keep moving, so you will need to make sure that he doesn't bump into anything.

Change the child who is blindfolded every few minutes. Because the game requires a lot of concentration it is better to stop after changing over a few times.

Musical ripples

Age range
Four to six.

Objective
To encourage control of sound.

What you need
A selection of different instruments.

What to do
Work with a small group if you have younger children or, with older ones, sort the class into small groups and give each group an instrument. The children in each group then form a circle and the child with the instrument makes the quietest sound she can with it and then passes the instrument on to the next child. This child has to make the same sound but a little

louder and the whole process is repeated until the instrument has gone right round the circle. The instrument can then be changed for another one to make a new sound or the game can be reversed by starting off with the loudest sound.

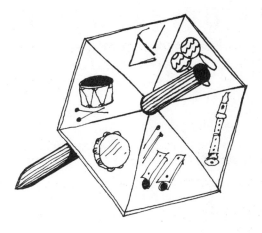

Spin a sound

Age range
Four to six.

Objective
To give experience in playing a variety of instruments in a variety of ways.

What you need
Two spinners and a selection of instruments.

What to do
Make two spinners, one showing pictures

59

of selected instruments and the other showing the words; fast/slow, loud/soft. The children then spin both spinners and when they land, find the instrument they need and play it in the way indicated by the spinner.

This activity is best done with a small group and it can be made easier or more difficult by varying the instructions on the spinners. Each child should have a chance to spin the spinners and play the instruments.

Keep to the rhythm

Age range
Five to six.

Objectives
To help develop discrimination and aural memory.

What you need
A selection of instruments and a tape-recorder.

What to do
Ask all the children to go out of the room except for you and one child. (You will need someone else to assist with those waiting.) Give the child left in the room an instrument and let her make up a simple rhythm. Ask the other children to come back into the room one at a time and let the child play her rhythm to the first child who then has to copy it as closely as possible to the next child called in. The rhythm is copied by each successive child until all the children are back in the room.

You can record all the events from start to finish and when the tape is played back the children will be able to tell if there are any differences between the rhythm played by the first child and that played by the last.

60

Making musical instruments

Chapter four

Creative activities involving making things are always popular with children. Making something that works is not only satisfying and exciting, but in the case of making musical instruments, useful as well. The children are involved in the production of sound before it becomes music and they are combining music with art and craft, science, language and maths.

Although full instructions are given for you to follow, experimenting is the key even with the youngest children. Make several instruments in a structured way so that the children closely follow instructions. Discuss what you are doing as you work together so that the children appreciate why you are doing a particular thing. Talk about how materials fix together and encourage them to make suggestions which you can try out and then assess the result.

Taking the instruments we have suggested as a starting point, try to design some for yourself. Be adventurous and innovative and don't be constrained by the usual shape of instruments, for instance, things which are blown don't have to be shaped like a tube.

There is so much potential for talking experience in activities of this kind. Guide the children into discussions about technical problems of construction and tie in early maths experience by talking about quantity, shape and weight. Discuss aesthetic questions of decoration and of course try out the instrument at every stage in its making. Discuss with the children how the sound is produced and what it is like, hard, soft, rattling, growling, tinkling, and really try to stretch descriptive vocabulary.

Let the children help you make instruments which involve difficult skills such as hammering or threading and do try to let all the children have experience of making several types of instrument and include some examples of these home-made instruments in the music corner.

Percussion

Sea shell glockenspiel

Age range
Five to six.

What you need
Strong shells of different sizes, a piece of wood about 15cm × 30cm or a wooden knife box, an assortment of beaters, PVA adhesive.

What to do
Using the beaters, let the children try out the sounds they can get from the various shells on different surfaces. Wood generally gives the best resonance for a base. They may find that they get a different quality of sound from different shells. They should then put them in order starting with the smallest sound and going to the largest; it will be a little difficult to order for pitch and this seems the most easily understood definition for young children at this point.

Stick the shells to the wooden base using a substantial amount of adhesive to bed them in and leave them until they are completely dry.

The adhesive does affect the sound to a small degree so an alternative is to put the shells in rows in a wooden knife box. The sides of the box give greater resonance to the sound too.

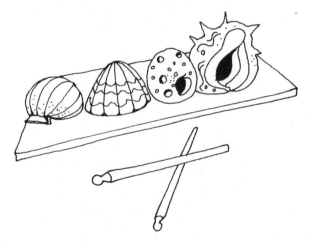

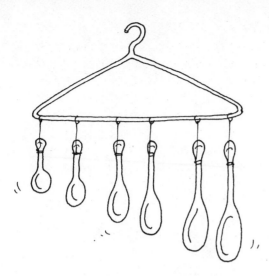

Spoon glockenspiel

Age range
Three to six.

What you need
A metal coat-hanger, six metal spoons of different sizes, strong thin thread, scissors, Blu-Tack.

What to do
Choose spoons which have a shaped handle so that the thread can be fixed round this and cut 30cm lengths of thread and let the children tie these to the handles of the spoons. They should then order the spoons according to size and tie them to the bottom of the coat-hanger, leaving equal spaces between. Make sure that the handle ends of the spoons are level, so that the size range can be easily seen. Cut off any loose ends and use a small piece of Blu-Tack to keep the thread in place on the coat-hanger.

Ask the children to test a variety of different beaters to see which is best depending on what sound they want to make. Hard wood and metal will give the most ringing sound.

Glock pots

Age range
Four to six.

What you need
About five earthenware plant pots of different sizes, string, 1m of dowelling, small saw, scissors, six baby milk cans, sand to fill two of them, sticky-back plastic or coloured paper and adhesive, Blu-Tack, sticky tape.

What to do
Make the stand by sticking with the sticky tape, the cans on top of each other to make two columns of three cans. Put sand in the two cans at the bottom of each column.

Cover each column with sticky-back plastic or sheets of coloured paper. Make the glocks by sawing the dowelling into one length of 50cm and five lengths of 6cm. Cut the string into five 50cm lengths and tie one of the little pieces of dowel to each. Thread each piece of string through the hole in a plant pot using the pieces of dowelling inside to make a stop. Tie the strings and the dangling pots to the long piece of dowelling making sure that they hang at different levels.

Put a large ball of Blu-Tack on each end of the long rod and press it down on to the two columns.

Use a piece of dowelling or another hard beater to play the glock pots.

Water chimes

Age range
Four to six.

What you need
An assortment of glass and plastic bottles and jars, an assortment of beaters, water, a shallow plastic tray.

What to do
Let the children experiment with the bottles, tapping them with different beaters to see what sounds are produced. They can then try filling them with different amounts of water and test the sounds made in the same way.

Usually glass vessels produce the best chiming sounds and different amounts of water will produce higher or lower notes. Ask the children to put about five vessels in order from highest to lowest notes or choose three or four whose sound appeals to them for any reason.

Put the chosen vessels on a plastic tray as a stand for playing.

Clip clops

Age range
Three to six.

What you need
An assortment of yoghurt pots and paint mixed with PVA adhesive.

What to do
Ask the children to decorate the pots using the paint and adhesive mix. Any bumps and lines will dry in relief so the pots will also be interesting to hold.

Then simply hold the base of a pot in each hand and tap the open end on to a table top. Let the children try tapping the open ends together too.

Hoof beats

Age range
Five to six.

What you need
A coconut, sandpaper, PVA adhesive or varnish, a saw, blunt knife.

What to do
Saw the coconut in half, trying to keep the edges level. Then chip out the kernel using a blunt knife. Smooth the outside of the shell with sandpaper and varnish or paint with PVA adhesive to get a satin finish.

   To play, either clop the open edges together while held in the hand or hold one in each hand and clop on to a table top.

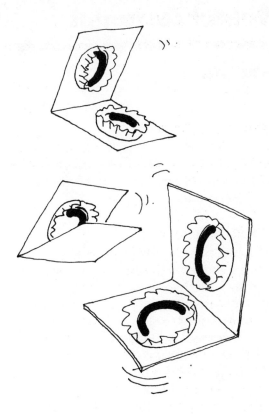

Claves

Age range
Three to six.

What you need
An old broom handle or dowelling, a saw, sandpaper.

What to do
Cut two pieces of the wood to a length of about 20cm and sandpaper the ends. Play by banging one rod on to the other in various rhythms.

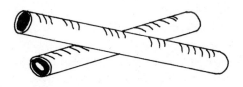

Card castanets

Age range
Four to six.

What you need
Small pieces of card, four metal bottle tops, adhesive, scissors.

What to do
Cut out two pieces of card about 12cm × 3cm and fold each in half across their length. Then stick two bottle tops on each half of the card so that they hit each other when the card is closed. You get a more definite sound if you fix them with the curly edge down, but you will need to wait for the adhesive to set firmly.

   Play the castanets by holding the card between fingers and thumb and tap together.

Walnut castanets

Age range
Five to six.

What you need
Four walnut shell halves, non-sticky plastic tape, contact adhesive (keep away from the children), latex adhesive and PVA adhesive.

What to do
Cut four strips of tape long enough to go round a thumb with about 4cm to spare. Then stick the two ends of the tape together leaving enough room for a thumb or finger to slip in. Children should not use contact adhesive so if they are to make these items use latex adhesive.

Stick the joined edge of the tape to the back of a walnut half and varnish the front of the shells with a coat of PVA adhesive or clear varnish.

To play, hold one shell by its loop in the finger or thumb of one hand and one in the other hand and tap together. Larger hands can hold one castanet on the forefinger and one on the thumb of one hand and tap together in the conventional way. In this case you can play with a pair in each hand.

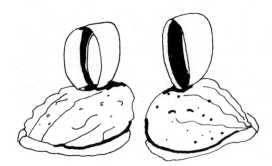

Cymbals

Age range
Three to six.

What you need
Two old saucepan lids about the same size, with handles; paint mixed with PVA adhesive.

What to do
The children can simply paint any design on to the top of the saucepan lids using the PVA paint mix to make it stick well. Play the cymbals by clashing them together or tie string round the handles and holding this bang the lid with a beater.

Japanese drum

Age range
Five to six.

What you need
A circular cardboard cheese box, two large wooden beads, fine string, art paper, felt-tipped pens or paints, rubber-based or quick drying adhesive.

What to do
Cut two pieces of string about 15cm long and knot one end of each and thread a bead on to each piece of string. Knot each string behind the bead. Now knot the string at the other end from the bead at 3cm less than the diameter of the box.

Take the bottom half of the cheese box and make two little cuts opposite each other in the edge of the box, for the string to sit in.

Make a further cut 1cm deep in the edge of the box between the first two cuts for the handle.

Take a piece of stiff art paper 15cm × 25cm and roll it into a tight tube 15cm long. Stick the edge down firmly and stick this into place in the cut you previously made, leaving about 2cm inside the box.

Put a blob of adhesive on the knots at the end of the string and put one in each of the cuts made for them.

Cut corresponding slits in the box lid and stick round the inside and fit this firmly over the base, pressing round the handle and strings to give a tidy finish.

The children can decorate the sides of the box using paints or felt-tipped pens. To play their drums the children should twist the handle quickly to make the beads bang on the box, one after the other.

Bongos

Age range
Three to four.

What you need
Two different-sized tins with plastic lids such as baby milk or coffee tins, coloured paper, quick drying adhesive, felt-tipped pens or paints, different coloured plastic electrical tape, bits of coloured transparent wrapping, bright beads, wool for threading, sticky-back plastic.

What to do
Wash out the tins and dry them thoroughly, putting the lids to one side. Talk to the children about how you would like to decorate the drum, whether to use pens or paints and what sort of 'design' to do. Decide whether to use the same colour paper to cover each drum. Then cut the paper so that it will wrap around the tin, allowing a little overlap. The children can then decorate the paper.

Put a clean piece of white paper on the table, so that you do not spoil the design, and spread adhesive evenly and thinly over the back of the sheets. A piece of card makes a good spreader. Place the tin on to the card and roll up the paper like a Swiss roll, making sure you stick the edge down well.

When the paper has dried in place, cover each drum with sticky-back plastic for extra durability. Stand the drums together and join them by winding round three strips of different coloured electrical tape, but do make sure that the bottoms of the drums are level so that they can sit on a surface without wobbling. All that needs to be done now is to put on the lids and have a go!

As a final touch, stick on circles of coloured transparent wrapping and possibly a string of bright beads too.

Rubbing board

Age range
Five to six.

What you need
A thick piece of wood about 25cm × 15cm, saw, sandpaper, a piece of dowelling as a scraper.

What to do
Using the saw, cut wedges about 1cm deep at intervals of about 3cm along the length of the wood. Sandpaper these until smooth and also smooth any other rough edges. To play this instrument run the piece of dowelling up and down the ridges or use a piece of card to give a flapping sound.

Sand rubbers

Age range
Three to six.

What you need
Two blocks of wood which can easily be held in the hand, coarse sandpaper, drawing pins or a staple gun.

What to do
Cut two pieces of sandpaper so that they are big enough to wrap round the blocks of wood lengthways. Wrap the sandpaper round tightly and fix in position using a stapler or drawing pins.
   To play, rub the blocks together to make a swishing sound.

Beaters

Age range
Three to six.

What you need
An assortment of sticks of different thicknesses, but about 30cm in length. They can be of different materials, plastic, wood or metal. Elastic bands of various thicknesses, corks, rubber bungs with holes, plastic and metal bottle tops, large wooden or plastic beads, ping-pong balls, old rubber balls, an assortment of adhesive, large, blunt pallet knives, old paint and hand brushes, soft or stiff art paper and cardboard tubes.

What to do
Use any metal sticks as they are, or stick bottle tops on to them. You can push holes in the ping-pong balls and cork and push sticks into them, or wind elastic bands round the end of a stick until you have a ball.

Make long hollow tubes from art paper. Use pallet knives, assorted brushes and cardboard tubes just as they are. These all make unusual sounds.

Bottle top shaker

Age range
Four to six.

What you need
A piece of broom handle about 25cm long or a piece of squared wood about the same size, flat topped 5cm nails, 10 or 12 metal bottle tops, sandpaper, hammer, piece of old wood, different coloured electrical tape.

What to do
Smooth any cut ends and edges of the broom handle with sandpaper and using the old piece of wood to nail on to, nail the bottle tops together in pairs, back to back. Then pull them out of the old piece of wood and nail each pair on to the broom handle, spacing them out along the length but leaving the end free to be held. Fix them in firmly but leave the bottle tops free to rattle loosely.

Wind different-coloured strips of electrical tape round the handle for decoration. You could also nail strips of ribbon or plastic tape on to the end to wave when the rattle is shaken.

Tin can shaker

Age range
Five to six.

What you need
A small baby milk can or coffee can, thin plastic covered wire, about 20 metal bottle tops, a hammer, nail, pliers, an old piece of wood, bits of coloured transparent wrapping adhesive, sticky-back plastic to cover the can or coloured paper.

What to do
Cover the can with sticky-back plastic or coloured paper. Then, using the old piece of wood as a backing for hammering, pierce three holes in the top lid edge of the can and three in the bottom, opposite each other.

Cut three lengths of wire about 20cm longer than the side of the can and tie a knot in the end of each of these.

Taking one wire at a time thread it through one of the holes in the bottom of the can so that the knot is on the inside. Make another knot on the outside of the can to keep it in place.

Punch holes in the bottle tops and thread five or six of these on to the wire.

Leaving the wire long enough to allow the tops to rattle, thread the end of the wire through the opposite top hole and tie into place, cutting off any loose ends. Then repeat this process with the other two wires.

The children can then decorate it using small twists of coloured transparent wrapping stuck in between the rows of bottle tops.

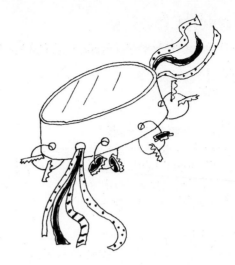

Tambourine

Age range
Five to six.

What you need
A large round margarine tub, an old piece of wood, pipe-cleaners, metal bottle tops, nails, a hammer, an old piece of wood, several pieces of different-coloured ribbon, adhesive.

What to do
Leaving a gap for a hand hold, mark out six places evenly spaced round the edge of the margarine tub. Then place the tub on the old piece of wood and nail through the plastic to make holes at the places marked.

Again using the old piece of wood as a base, make holes in the bottle tops. Thread three or four of these on to each of the six pipe-cleaners and thread one end of each pipe-cleaner through a hole in the tub and then twist the ends together to form a loop on which the bottle tops rattle loosely.

Either make a further two holes in the tub or use adhesive to fix ribbons on each side of the tambourine for decoration.

Sleigh bells

Age range
Five to six.

What you need
Piece of broom handle about 10cm long, piece of old wood, hammer, thin 5cm nails, 35cm of stiff wire, contact adhesive, eight metal bottle tops.

What to do
Make holes in all the bottle tops with the hammer and nails, using the old piece of wood to nail into. Then thread the bottle tops on to the wire and make sure they rattle freely.

To make the handle, make a hole about 3cm deep in each end of the piece of broom handle using a nail and dip one end of the wire into the contact adhesive, let it set and then push it firmly into one of the holes in the handle. Finally, bend the wire round in a loop and fix the loose end into the other hole on the handle.

Maraca pots

Age range
Three to six.

What you need
Two yoghurt pots, different-coloured electrical tape, peas, rice and lentils.

What to do
Put a small amount of the dried items in one pot and stick the other pot on top using a strip of brightly coloured electrical tape.

Cut small squares of different-coloured electrical tape and use them to decorate the maracas.

Make two maracas and put different dried items in each.

Bottle maracas

Age range
Three to six.

What you need
Two small clear plastic bottles with narrow necks and screw tops, lentils, paint mixed with PVA adhesive.

What to do
Put enough lentils into each bottle to make a pleasing sound when shaken and fix the tops of the bottles on tightly.

Decorate the bottles with PVA paint mix.

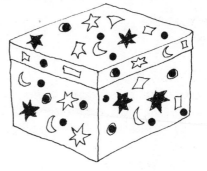

Metal maracas

Age range
Three to six.

What you need
Metal cocoa tin with lid, an assortment of fillers (for example, rice, sand or dried peas), electrical tape, adhesive shapes.

What to do
Wash the tin and strip off the paper sleeve. Then decorate it with strips of different-coloured electrical tape in bands or stripes and complete it by adding adhesive shapes to make a pattern.

Let the children try out several different fillers and test the sound of each. They will get a different sound quality from different quantities of filler so they can experiment with this too.

Discuss the sounds with the children and select sounds which are most pleasing for whatever reason. Some children may like a loud crackling sound and some may prefer a softer swishing sound. Talk about personal preferences and sounds to produce certain effects, for example, the sound of hailstones on the window pane.

Fool's hammer

Age range
Four to six.

What you need
One sheet of activity paper, a length of wool, adhesive tape, a medium-sized paper bag, dried peas, felt-tipped pens.

What to do
Tell the children to put a handful of peas in a paper bag and blow it up, screw the neck tightly and tie it up with wool.

Working diagonally, they should then roll up the sheet of activity paper into a tight stick and secure the end with adhesive tape. Cut the stick so that it is about 30cm long and tie the other end of the wool to it, securing the wool in place with adhesive tape (make the length from the bag to the stick only about 20cm).

To play this instrument, the children should shake the stick. The paper bag can be decorated with the child's name and other patterns using felt-tipped pens.

Swoosher

Age range
Three to six.

What you need
A long cardboard tube, rice, thin card, electrical tape, felt-tipped pens, 30cm strips of different-coloured tissue-paper.

What to do
Ask the children to cut a circle of card bigger than the end of the tube and slit round the edge with scissors so that it can be bent over the end of the tube. Fix one end in place with the electrical tape and

then the children can put a handful of rice in the tube. They can test how much to put in by putting their hand over the open end and tipping the tube backwards and forwards to hear what sort of a swoosh they get, and then adjusting the amount of rice accordingly. Once they have the sound they like they can fix the card over the open end.

Ask the children to decorate the tube using felt-tipped pens and tassels of tissue-paper fixed to the centre which will wave as they swoosh.

Slosher

Age range
Three to six.

What you need
A large, long plastic bottle with top, paint mixed with PVA adhesive, water.

What to do
Get the children to quarter fill the bottle with water and then fix the top firmly. They can then decorate with stripes or waves in different-coloured PVA paints.

To play, simply turn the bottle from side to side to get a swishing noise or shake up and down for a slosh.

Wind

Bottle flutes

Age range
Five to six.

What you need
A selection of glass and plastic bottles, water.

What to do
Ask the children to try blowing over the top of different bottles to see whether they can obtain a sound. The flow of air needs to be at right angles to the top of the bottle to achieve a good sound. Put different amounts of water in the bottles and let them blow again. The water will effectively alter the space in the bottle and consequently the sound produced by blowing over it. Pick out four or five bottles of the same size and put water in each, increasing the amount in each successive bottle. The children should find that the note produced varies according to the amount of water. Bottles with long necks produce the best notes, but do experiment to find sounds the children like best.

Pipes

Age range
Five to six.

What you need
Paper drinking straws, scissors, a thick needle.

What to do
Flatten the end of a drinking straw and cut off the corners at an angle.

Pierce a hole in the straw anywhere along the length of the straw using the needle. If you make several pipes you can change the position of the hole so that the children can hear how this effects the sound produced.

The children should blow down the cut end to play the pipes.

Tube trumpet

Age range
Four to six.

What you need
Length of flexible plastic tube (approximately 1m) and a funnel to fit into the end.

What to do
Fix the funnel into the end of the tube.

To play, the children should blow down the tube end.

Try different lengths and different diameters of tubing to alter the sound.

Comb and paper

Age range
Five to six.

What you need
A small narrow-toothed comb and a piece of tissue-paper.

What to do
Fold the tissue-paper in half and place the top of the comb inside the fold of the paper.

To play, the children should place the fold-covered edge of the comb just inside the lips, keeping the lips slightly apart and sing 'Der, der, der' to the tune of their choice.

Kazoo

Age range
Three to four.

What you need
Cardboard rolls of different lengths and diameter, tissue-paper, elastic bands and a pencil.

What to do
Cut a 15cm square of tissue-paper, cover the end of a cardboard tube with the tissue-paper and fix with an elastic band, making sure that the paper is taut, but not about to tear. Then push a hole in the tube with a sharp pencil, about half way along. Now let the children sing into the kazoo. They should fit their lips into the open end and sing 'Der, der' to the tune of their choice.

Bubbler

Age range
Three to six.

What you need
A bucket of water, a length of hose, a small plastic container of water, a straw.

What to do
Using either combination of tube and container, depending on the volume of sound required, the children simply blow through the tube into the water to produce a bubbling sound.

This can be used as a sound effect or as an accompaniment to a song, but for regular 'beats' it will need a fair degree of breath control.

Strings

Tin guitar

Age range
Three to six.

What you need
Large coffee tin or baby milk tin, a selection of large elastic bands, coloured electrical tape, coloured paper and adhesive, or sticky-back plastic.

What to do
Either cover the can with a piece of coloured paper or sticky-back plastic. Then select four or five elastic bands which will stretch over the tin lengthways and produce a resonant sound when twanged.

Pull the elastic bands together about half way down one side and fix them to the side of the can with a small piece of electrical tape.

Do the same on the opposite side. Using a long piece of the tape wind it right round the can to cover the holding tapes and to add decoration.

Box guitar

Age range
Three to six.

What you need
A cardboard shoe-box, five strong elastic bands, a thin piece of wood about 10cm long, scissors, felt-tipped pens or paints.

What to do
Cover or paint out any labels on the box and let the children decorate the sides using felt-tipped pens or paints. Then cut a round hole approximately 8cm in diameter in the centre of the lid. Put the lid on the box and stretch the elastic bands round the box lengthways, but evenly spaced across the sound hole.

Position the piece of wood under the 'strings' at one end to give them extra tension.

Household goods selection

Age range
Three to six.

What you need
Corrugated plastic tubing, child safety gate, dowelling, clear acetate film, metal tray, brush, dustbin, dustbin lid, saucepans, tins, boxes.

What to do
This selection of instruments can be made from different household items, with no alteration.

Blooter
A piece of corrugated plastic tubing, about 1m in length. This is played by whirling it around the head or in a circle at arms length. It produces a whooping, bubbly noise not unlike the sound 'bloo', in different tones.

Brick-a-brac
An old child safety gate in wood or metal. This is played by running a piece of dowelling or a ruler up and down the rails.

Scruncher
Any thin acetate film wrapping; played by simply scrunching it in the hand.

Cymbals
An old metal tray which is held and stroked with a soft or hard hand brush. To get a gong-like effect drill a hole in each corner of the tray and suspend it from a convenient place and beat it with a hard item.

Big bass drum

A plastic or metal dustbin (preferably one used for storage of toys etc and not waste). This is played by standing it on its end and beating it with the hands or a beater.

Steel band

One or two metal dustbin lids, placed inverted in a plastic bin or simply on the ground. They are best played with a wood or metal beater.

Drum kit

Several pans and buckets and tins, both metal and plastic, and boxes made of card or wood. These can be arranged around the musician in any order and played with a variety of beaters.

Singing

Chapter five

For many children the first experience of making music is when they sing nursery rhymes and action songs with their parents. Children learn to speak by imitating the words they hear and likewise they develop control of the voice by singing songs and repeating rhymes.

In the classroom, singing can help to develop the children's musical abilities and social skills and it also acts as a valuable aid in the development of language and reading. It can stimulate and help to develop the bond between the teacher and children as they join together in a controlled and enjoyable activity.

It is important that singing should be relaxed and enjoyable but at the same time singing should not become sloppy or as can so easily happen, become an excuse for shouting as the children become over enthusiastic or excited.

Although children have high voices, the pitch at which they can comfortably sing is much lower. After several attempts with daily or frequent singing you will be able to identify their range and be able to pitch most songs correctly, especially if you don't worry about accompaniment at first.

Most children can sing, very few are tone deaf but some children take a little longer to learn to place their voices. Always encourage them to keep their interest and with some individual attention their confidence and their singing ability will grow. Regular singing sessions will help develop the children's sense of pitch and the relationship between one sound and another.

Always the emphasis should be on enjoyment, and a willingness to experiment.

Choosing songs

Apart from playing singing games, which are fun and develop certain skills, singing songs for their own sake is also a major part of the music curriculum.

When choosing songs it is well to remember certain points:
● The children should like the song. It could be the rhythm or the tune which attracts them and if they can remember it easily they will enjoy singing it.
● Younger children in general like repetition and pattern in each verse and the shorter the song the better.
● Songs with a chorus encourage the children to join in.
● Action songs provide a dramatic element in their movement, give added enjoyment and are usually easier to learn.
● Make sure that the words are within the comprehension of the children and that the range of notes is not too wide.

Avoid songs with very high or very low notes.

Songs can be chosen for all sorts of reasons; to link with changing seasons, topic work, or children's own personal favourites. However, as with any subject it is best not to introduce too many new songs at once.

Lots of children are already familiar with nursery rhymes and they are a good basis on which to build.

Question and answer songs are always popular because the children feel involved and they can be sung by two groups of children, one to sing the question and the other to sing the reply. For example:
● 'Mary, Mary quite contrary';
● 'There's a hole in my bucket';
● 'Baa Baa black sheep';
● 'Do you know the muffin man?';
● 'Where is thumbkin?'.

Repetitive songs also enable children to make up their own words fairly easily. Encourage this by taking a well-known song and changing one or two words. For example, in 'The wheels on the bus' the youngest children will be able to think of many types of passengers for the bus. Older children can have fun trying to fit different words to a well-known tune.

Songs which **build up and add an extra verse** are excellent for developing auditory memory, for example:
- 'One finger, one thumb keep moving';
- 'Old Macdonald had a farm';
- 'The twelve days of Christmas';
- 'There was an old woman who swallowed a fly'.

With young children it is best to start off with only a few additions but a frieze or pictures will help to prompt their memories and add to the enjoyment of the song.

Counting songs are a great help in building mathematical concepts and can be used with counters and number flash cards. Try songs which count forwards such as:
- 'This old man';
- 'One for sorrow, two for joy';
- 'One potato, two potato'.

Songs which count backwards include:
- 'Ten green bottles';
- 'Five little speckled frogs';
- 'Five little ducks went swimming one day';
- 'Ten fat sausages';
- 'Five currant buns in a baker's shop';
- 'Five little pumpkins'.

Finally 'One man went to mow' counts backwards and forwards in each verse.

Lots of **traditional singing games** are also enjoyed by children and these can be played almost anywhere. If the group is large, some children can play while others watch but they can all join in with the singing. These games can help develop self-discipline, social co-operation and a sense of rhythm and pitch. The body movements and actions are geared to the music and the children can cope easily with the simple tunes. For example:
- 'Ring a ring o' roses';
- 'The big ship sailed through the alley alley O';
- 'In and out the fairy bluebells';
- 'Oranges and lemons';
- 'The farmer's in his den'.

Teaching new songs

When teaching new songs it is a good idea to know the song well yourself, so that you can sing it without using copies of the words. The important thing is to encourage all the children to join in, especially the shy ones. The children will be more willing to join in with you singing, rather than with a tape-recorder. Once they begin to use their voices regularly their confidence and singing skills will develop.

Group the children around you and in a few words introduce the song and sing it all the way through. When singing, sing directly to the children, looking at them so that they can absorb all the words and the tune. If there is a repetitive part to the song then the children will probably pick that part up first and join in.

Songs for the youngest children should be very simple, short and repetitive. The action songs in *This Little Puffin . . .* compiled by Elizabeth Matterson (Puffin) and in *Counting Songs* and *Action Songs* (Early Learning Centre) are ideal for this purpose.

Visual clues are good teaching aids but it is best to teach only one or two verses at any one time and build up the song gradually. With songs that do not have much repetition, the easiest and quickest way, once the song has been introduced, is to get the children to echo you as you sing each line. Link lines together and then try to sing a whole verse. Only teach one verse at a time, but keep singing the rest of the verses so that continuity and interest is maintained and the session is musically satisfying. It is also a good idea to try only one new song each session and then go on to familiar ones which the children enjoy. Get groups of children to sing verses in turn and accompany with clapping to keep the time going. If children can't remember the words they can always hum or sing 'la, la, la', until they get to a familiar bit.

Use every opportunity you can to sing with your children until it becomes quite the natural thing to do when you have a spare ten minutes. Encourage the children to enjoy themselves and to be relaxed. As you build up your repertoire there will be lots of occasions when it will be fun to sing an appropriate song which perfectly captures the essence of the moment.

Sing out . . . sing out

Age range
Five to six.

Objectives
To identify, and to produce loud and soft sounds.

What you need
A blindfold.

What to do
Ask the children to sit or stand in a circle. Blindfold one of the children who then stands in the middle of the circle.

Choose different children to sing loudly, softly or in an ordinary voice and pick one to use a very loud voice. Now take the blindfold off the child.

All the children should now sing one note (give them the note yourself) and those that have been picked by you should sing in the way they have been asked. The child in the centre should now try to identify the loudest singer and tap her on the shoulder. They then change places and you can change the singing roles for the next round.

The game can be varied by choosing the child who sings the softest, lowest, fastest or slowest etc.

Missing words

Age range
Three to six.

Objectives
To develop concentration and auditory memory.

What you need
No special requirements.

What to do
This is a singing game with actions so the children will need to learn the following song:
'My hat it has three corners,
Three corners has my hat,
If it had not three corners
It would not be my hat.'
The following actions accompany the song and it is best to learn both simultaneously:
- My – point to self;
- hat – flat hands with fingertips pointing over head;
- three – hold up three fingers;
- corners – draw a corner with the forefinger;
- had not – shake head;
- would not – shake finger.

Sing the song with the actions a few times then miss out single words but continue to do the actions. Next miss out two words, for example, corners and hat.

Follow-up
Teach the children other action songs.

Hum that tune

Age range
Three to six.

Objectives
Memory training and matching.

What you need
No special requirements

What to do
Sit with the children in a circle and start off by humming a line or two from a well-known nursery rhyme, song or even a television programme. See if the children can guess what the song is. Try to make sure that you hum tunefully and quite loudly. You can then let the children take turns at humming and encourage them to pick a song which hasn't been done that session.

Follow-up
The children could hum the next bit of a song or as much or as little as they can remember, with or without guessing the title.

Finish the song

Age range
Four to six.

Objective
A fun way of learning and remembering songs.

What you need
No special requirements.

What to do
Sit with the children in a circle and ask one child to start to sing a song, singing the first line only. This is quite difficult at first unless the song is fairly repetitious like 'John Brown's body'. You can help by making the children keep their eyes on you so that you can signal when the line has finished and the next child should start.

Ask the next child to sing the second line and the next one the third line and so on. This goes on until someone can't sing their line, then you can supply it and round it off by everyone singing the whole song. The one who couldn't sing a line then has a go at starting off the next song.

Change your mind

Age range
Five to six.

Objective
Free singing.

What you need
No special requirements.

What to do
Tell everybody to choose a well-known song but they must keep it secret. Then at a given sign everyone walks about, criss-crossing around the room and singing their own song as loudly as possible, without shouting. The idea of the game is that they are to try to encourage the others to change their song to the one they are singing.

After a little while ask everyone to stop and you can then find out who has managed to get the biggest group of children to sing their song, or which is the most popular song of the day.

Noah's ark

Age range
Three to six.

Objective
Memory training for tunes.

What you need
No special requirements.

What to do
Choose a simple song which the children all know such as 'Twinkle, twinkle little star' and sing it all the way through. Then have a go at singing the tune of the song but using the words 'Miaow, miaow, miaow'. The children will soon get the hang of this.

Next divide the children into groups of about three or four and ask each group to think of a different animal sound such as 'woof', 'moo' or 'oink'. Each group then has to see whether they can sing the chosen song with their sound.

With older children you can extend this by letting each group take it in turns to sing just one line of the song as you point to them and the aim is to sing in the correct time and tune, but with their own sound. Do let the groups swap sounds and change songs too.

Hunt the song

Age range
Five to six.

Objectives
To help aural discrimination and matching.

What you need
Paper or pictures, pencils.

What to do
Choose three popular nursery rhymes or songs and write each one on a piece of paper so that there are enough for each of the children in the class to have one piece of paper. If the children cannot read, substitute a picture and make sure they know which picture represents which song. Then fold the slips of paper, put them in a hat or box and shake them up. Let each child pick one. When all the children have seen which song they have picked they should walk about the room singing the song. As they walk they have to sing and listen, because when they hear someone else singing the same song they have to join hands with them, but keep on singing and walking round until three big groups are formed.

Song jigsaw

Age range
Five to six.

Objectives
To develop memory and sequencing.

What you need
No special requirements.

What to do
Choose a well-known song which the children all know and give one line of the song to each child. For example, for 'Hickory dickory dock' you will need five children and one extra child who should stand away from the group. The other five children then begin to walk about the room repeating their own line, while the sixth child has to listen carefully and find out which of the children is singing the first line. Once this has been discovered the child singing the first line is to stand at the front. This is repeated until all five children are standing in the correct order to sing the song.

When the last child is in place they stop singing and then at a signal from you they each sing their line in the order which the searcher has placed them. The rest of the class must listen to see if the song is correct.

Follow-up
This game can be made more difficult with a longer song.

Sing a round

Age range
Five to six.

Objectives
To develop concentration, and to enjoy a new sound.

What you need
No special requirements.

What to do
Singing a 'round' is quite an old device for musical amusement. Pick very short songs with happy tunes and split the class into two groups. It may be as well to move them apart in the room at first.

Start one group off singing and then start the second group off as the first reaches the end of the first line. 'Row, row, row your boat' is a good song for this.

Tell the children to concentrate on their own words while singing and not to listen to the other group at first. With practice older children can listen to the other group as they sing and enjoy the double sound.

Choose songs such as:
- 'Row, row, row your boat';
- 'Frère Jacques';
- 'Polly put the kettle on';
- 'London's burning';
- 'My hat it has three corners'.

Resources

Chapter six

Making a music corner

If you have enough space a music corner is a valuable addition to the classroom. With younger children the best place to site one is very near to their own working area. However, it is very much a personal choice and largely determined by the physical structure of the building. It should be as far away as possible from areas of heavy traffic and it is a good idea to have some kind of screen to protect the rest of the children from some of the sound and to encourage concentration.

When setting up the corner try to collect a good variety of instruments. However, it is a good idea to start off with only a few instruments and gradually extend the scope with more bought ones and some home-made ones.

Include instruments like:
- shakers;
- tambourines;
- woodblocks;
- triangles;
- bells;
- clappers;
- chime bars (C D E F G A B C' D' E' and also F# and Bb);
- beaters (felt, rubber, metal) wooden or;
- home-made instruments, like drums, kazoo, paper and comb (see Chapter 4).

A tape-recorder is also useful and if possible a small table and a collection of containers of different sizes are very practical. Store most of the instruments under the table and have a selected few at a time out on top for use. Use decorated coffee tins, large plastic ice-cream cartons, rectangular washing-up bowls or plastic vegetable storage racks to put the instruments in. If you have a storage unit which has side drawers these can be used to hold workcards, music books, chime bars etc.

Try to incorporate a display board and a working surface so that the children have a visual stimulus and a place to work on with the instruments.

It is best to limit the number of children who can use the corner at any one time and be aware of the noise level when working close to other people. If this is a problem, encourage quiet activities as often as possible and provide 'small-sound' instruments such as triangles, castanets, soft shakers, sand blocks and little bells.

Try to plan in advance so that the children's activities sometimes arise out of other areas of the curriculum. Give them short, specific tasks or give time for free experiment and time to repeat activities. It may be worthwhile to re-position the music corner from time to time, so that the direction of sound can be changed. Such changes of scene are also often novel and refreshing for the children.

Audio visual resources

Recorded music, radio and television are all valuable sources for teaching ideas in the classroom. They can be used to provide music for movement, songs, games and as a way of encouraging listening skills and aesthetic awareness.

There is a wealth of music broadcast every day on the radio, from numerous stations, and in the various television regions which can be used. The BBC and ITV schools programmes are best taped or videoed so that you are not tied to a programme time and they can then be stored and used to best advantage later. Another obvious advantage is the ability to stop, start and rewind so that bits of programmes can be explained or heard again. The tapes should be labelled clearly and stored.

It is a good idea to make a collection of short musical pieces on tape for permanent use with the children. These should be examples of different instruments or types of music. Tape only short pieces of music, snatches of good melody or rhythm from longer pieces and choose examples of different ethnic origin and as many styles and historical periods as possible, for example, Elizabethan lute, flute and tabor, 1960s folk, brass bands, Glenn Miller's orchestra, reggae, rapping, Handel's strings, Indian and Chinese music and so on. If the children hear pieces a few times and they are sufficiently stimulating and interesting they will soon get to know them well.

Try to build up a collection of music with strong story lines such as:
- *Peter and the Wolf* by Prokofiev;
- *The Nutcracker Suite* by Tchaikovsky;
- *The Sorcerer's Apprentice* by Dukas;
- *Petrushka* by Stravinsky.
The sound tracks from some Walt Disney films are also good examples of more modern music on these lines, for example:
- *Dumbo*;
- *The Wizard of Oz*;
- *Mary Poppins*;
- *Jungle Book*.
Walt Disney also produce *Fantasia* which is a cartoon illustration of a collection of music, mostly classical, all stirring.

Some music is suitable for topic work,

and parents may be willing to lend recordings; or failing that, your local library may have an audio loans system.

Listed here are a selection of areas of study which may be used by younger children and music which can be used as an extra dimension to the topic.

Water
- *Submerged Cathedral* by Debussy;
- *Fingal's Cave* by Mendelssohn;
- *The Flying Dutchman* by Wagner;
- *Water Music* by Handel;
- *Trout Quintet* by Schubert.

Animals
- *Firebird* by Stravinsky;
- *Flight of the Bumble Bee* by Rimsky-Korsakov;
- *Carnival of the Animals* by Saint-Saëns;
- *Jungle Book* (Walt Disney);
- *Fantasia* (Wat Disney);
- *Dumbo* (Walt Disney).

Parades and marches
- *Radetsky March* by Strauss I;
- *The Luftwaffe March* by R. Goodwin;
- Any collection of brass band marches.

Space
- *Planets Suite* by Holst;
- *Dr Who* by the BBC Radiophonic workshop;
- *2001 . . . a Space Odyssey* film theme (*Also Sprock Zarathustra* by Richard Strauss).

Circuses and fairs
- 'Dance of the Tumblers' from *The Snowmaiden* by Rimsky-Korsakov;
- *Circus Polka* by Stravinsky;
- *Radetsky March* by Strauss I;
- *Entry of the Gladiators* by Julius Fučik.

Weather and the seasons
- *Rite of Spring* by Stravinsky;

- *Four Seasons* by Vivaldi;
- 'Waltz of the snow flakes' from *The Nutcracker Suite* by Tchaikovsky.

Toys
- *Toy Symphony* by Haydn;
- *La Boutique Fantastique* by Rossini;
- *Golliwog's Cakewalk* by Debussy.

Mechanical things
- Symphony 101, *Clock* by Haydn;
- *Thirty-two Pieces for Mechanical Clocks* by Haydn.

Trombone
- *Pulcinella* by Stravinsky;
- *In the Mood* by Glenn Miller.

Strings
- *Pizzicato Polka* by Strauss II;
- Any music by Mantovani.

Violin
- *Violin Concerto* by Sibelius.

Flute
- Any music by James Galway.

Cello
- 'The Swan' from *Carnival of the Animals* played by Julian Lloyd Webber.

Double Bass
- 'The Elephant' from *Carnival of the Animals*.

Oboe
- 'Fairy of the Crystal Fountain' from *The Nutcracker Suite*.

Clarinet
- *Clarinet Concerto* by Mozart.

French Horn
- *Horn Concerto* by Mozart.

Harp
- *Flute and Harp Concerto* by Mozart;
- Irish folk music.

Tuba
- *Pictures at an Exhibition* by Mussorgsky.

Xylophone
- 'Fossils' from *Carnival of the Animals* by Saint-Saëns.

Castanets
- *España* by Chabrier;
- Spanish folk music.

Guitar
- Music by John Williams, The Beatles, or Max Boyce.

Drums
- Any jazz or military band music.

Piano
- *Minute Waltz* by Chopin.

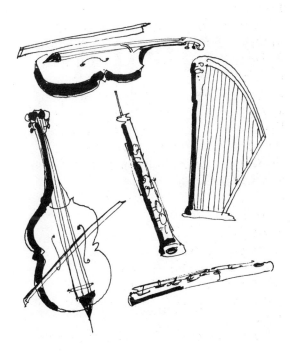

Musical terms for the complete beginner

For those of you who don't read music or play the piano:

• This is where you will find middle C on the piano. This is the C nearest the middle of the instrument, almost in line with the keyhole.

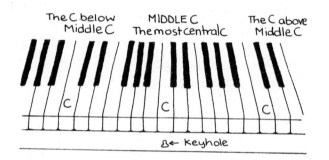

• Here are the names of the other white notes near middle C and which you will find in most common, simple nursery rhymes and songs.

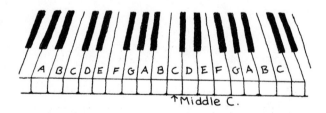

• Music is written on groups of five lines (and four spaces) called *staves*.

For the piano there are staves for the right and left hands, each with its own sign:

This is the right hand stave, which usually shows the tune:

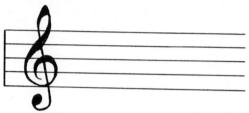

Its sign is called a *treble clef*.

This is the left hand stave which usually shows an accompaniment:

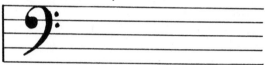

Its sign is called a *bass clef*.

Both staves are usually linked by a *brace*

The end of a tune is marked with two lines like this:

These are the notes you would probably need, to pick out a simple tune on the piano or glockenspiel. They are on the upper stave, preceded by the treble clef. Some are on lines and some are in spaces:

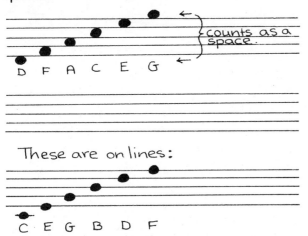

These are on lines:

C E G B D F

Middle C actually falls on a line between the two staves. Too many lines would be confusing so notes below the stave are written on small lines called ledger lines.

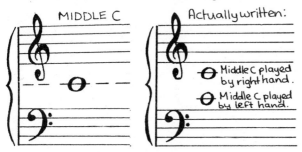

There are different types of notes which last for varying lengths of time; here is a simplified explanation:

A crochet lasts for one beat, ♩
A minim lasts for two beats, ♩
A dotted minim lasts for three beats, ♩.
A semibreve lasts for four beats, 𝅝
A quaver lasts for half a beat, ♫
The *time signature* is the *rhythm* or *beat* of the tune and is shown by numbers at the beginning, after the *treble clef*.

4
4 or C (= common time) means 4 beats in a bar, 1, 2, 3, 4

3
4 means 3 beats in a bar, 1, 2, 3
There are many other time signatures but they require a more complex explanation.

Bars
The music is divided into sections by a bar line. Within each bar is the value of notes which make up the number of beats given in the time signature.

Sharps and flats
The black keys on the piano sound sharper or flatter than the purer notes, the white keys.

When sharps or flats are needed in the music these signs are used: *b* (flat) or # (sharp).

In many simple songs such as nursery rhymes the most common sharps and flats are: B*b* and F#.

The *b* or # sign is always written before the *time signature* on the *line* or *space* of the note in question and indicates that all these notes in the tune are *b* or #, for example:

Here are some of the *b* or # notes on the piano:

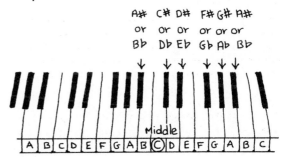

Accompanying songs, pages 51 and 52

Ostinati with one note

Lavender's blue

Ostinati

Lav - en - der's blue, did -dle, did -dle, Lav - en - der's green;

When I am king, did - dle, did - dle, You shall be queen

London Bridge

Ostinati

Lon - don Bridge is fal - ling down, Fal - ling down, fal - ling down,

Lon - don Bridge is fal - ling down, My fair la - dy.

London's burning

Ostinati

Lon-don's burn-ing, Lon-don's burn-ing, Fetch the en - gines, Fetch the en - gines

Frère Jacques

Ostinati

Frè - re Jac - ques, Frè - re Jac - ques, Dor -mez vous? Dor - mez vous?

Ostinati with two notes

Bobby Shafto

Three blind mice

One, two, three, four, five

Oranges and lemons
Ostinati

C'   C'   C'   C'

C'   A   C'   A   F   G   A   B♭   G   C'   A   F   C'
Oran - ges and le - mons, Say the bells of St Cle - ment's. You

C'   C'   C'

C'   A   C'   A   F   G   A   B♭   G   C'   A   F
owe me five far - things, Say the bells of St Mar - tin's.

G   G   G   G

G   E   G   E   C   D   E   F   D   G   E   C
When will you pay me? Say the bells of Old Bai - ley.

Ostinati with three notes

Twinkle twinkle
Ostinati

D   G   A   D   G   A   D   G   A   D   G   A

D   D   A   A   A   G   G   F   G   A   F   D   A   A
Twin-kle, twin - kle, lit - tle star, How I won - der what you are,

There's a hole in my bucket
Ostinati

G   G   G

G   A   B   D   D   E   G   D   E   G   D
1. There's a hole in my buck - et, dear Li - za, dear

G   G   G   C   D   G

E   G   G   A   B   D   D   E   G   D   E   G   F♯   G
Li - za, There's a hole in my buck - et, dear Li - za, a hole.